PLAY ON SHAKESPEARE

Macbeth

D0556954

PLAY ON SHAKESPEARE

All's Well That Ends Well	Virginia Grise
Antony and Cleopatra	Christopher Chen
As You Like It	David Ivers
The Comedy of Errors	Christina Anderson
Coriolanus	Sean San José
Cymbeline	Andrea Thome
Edward III	Octavio Solis
Hamlet	Lisa Peterson
Henry IV	Yvette Nolan
Henry V	Lloyd Suh
Henry VI	Douglas P. Langworthy
Henry VIII	Caridad Svich
Julius Caesar	Shishir Kurup
King John	Brighde Mullins
King Lear	Marcus Gardley
Love's Labour's Lost	Josh Wilder
Macbeth	Migdalia Cruz
Measure for Measure	Aditi Brennan Kapil
The Merchant of Venice	Elise Thoron
The Merry Wives of Windsor	Dipika Guha
A Midsummer Night's Dream	Jeffrey Whitty
Much Ado About Nothing	Ranjit Bolt
Othello	Mfoniso Udofia
Pericles	Ellen McLaughlin
Richard II	Naomi Iizuka
Richard III	Migdalia Cruz
Romeo and Juliet	Hansol Jung
The Taming of the Shrew	Amy Freed
The Tempest	Kenneth Cavander
Timon of Athens	Kenneth Cavander
Titus Andronicus	Amy Freed
Troilus and Cressida	Lillian Groag
Twelfth Night	Alison Carey
The Two Gentlemen of Verona	Amelia Roper
The Two Noble Kinsmen	Tim Slover
The Winter's Tale	Tracy Young

Macbeth

by
William Shakespeare

Modern verse translation by
Migdalia Cruz

Dramaturgy by
Ishia Bennison

Arizona Center
for Medieval and
Renaissance Studies
ACMRS PRESS
Arizona State University
Tempe, Arizona
2021

Publication of Play On Shakespeare is assisted by
generous support from the Hitz Foundation.
For more information, please visit www.playonshakespeare.org

Published by ACMRS Press
Arizona Center for Medieval and Renaissance Studies,
Arizona State University, Tempe, Arizona
www.acmrspress.com

Library of Congress Cataloging-in-Publication Data
Names: Cruz, Migdalia, author. | Bennison, Ishia, dramaturge. | Shake-
   speare, William, 1564-1616. Macbeth.
Title: Macbeth / by William Shakespeare ; modern verse translation by
   Migdalia Cruz ; dramaturgy by Ishia Bennison.
Description: Tempe, Arizona : ACMRS Press, 2021. | Series: Play on
   Shakespeare | Summary: "In Migdalia Cruz's Macbeth, the Witches
   run the world. The Macbeths live out a dark cautionary tale of love,
   greed, and power, falling from glory into calamity as the Witches spin
   their fate. Translating Shakespeare's language for a modern audience,
   Nuyorican playwright Migdalia Cruz rewrites Macbeth with all the
   passion of the Bronx"-- Provided by publisher.
Identifiers: LCCN 2021001978 (print) | LCCN 2021001979 (ebook) | ISBN
   9780866986601 (paperback) | ISBN 9780866986632 (ebook)
Subjects: LCSH: Macbeth, King of Scotland, active 11th century--Drama.
Classification: LCC PR2878.M3 C78 2021 (print) | LCC PR2878.M3
   (ebook) | DDC 812/.54--dc23
LC record available at https://lccn.loc.gov/2021001978
LC ebook record available at https://lccn.loc.gov/2021001979

Printed in the United States of America

We wish to acknowledge our gratitude
for the extraordinary generosity of the
Hitz Foundation

∼

Special thanks to the Play on Shakespeare staff
Lue Douthit, CEO/Creative Director
Kamilah Long, Managing Director
Taylor Bailey, Associate Creative Director
Summer Martin, Director of Learning Engagement
Katie Kennedy, Publications Project Manager
Jacourtney Mountain-Bluhm, Executive Assistant

∼

Originally commissioned by the
Oregon Shakespeare Festival
Bill Rauch, Artistic Director
Cynthia Rider, Executive Director

SERIES PREFACE
PLAY ON SHAKESPEARE

In 2015, the Oregon Shakespeare Festival announced a new commissioning program. It was called "Play on!: 36 playwrights translate Shakespeare". It elicited a flurry of reactions. For some people this went too far: "You can't touch the language!". For others, it didn't go far enough: "Why not new adaptations?" I figured we would be on the right path if we hit the sweet spot in the middle.

Some of the reaction was due not only to the scale of the project, but its suddenness: 36 playwrights, along with 38 dramaturgs, had been commissioned and assigned to translate 39 plays, and they were already hard at work on the assignment. It also came fully funded by the Hitz Foundation with the shocking sticker price of $3.7 million.

I think most of the negative reaction, however, had to do with the use of the word "translate." It's been difficult to define precisely. It turns out that there is no word for the kind of subtle and rigorous examination of language that we are asking for. We don't mean "word for word," which is what most people think of when they hear the word translate. We don't mean "paraphrase," either.

The project didn't begin with 39 commissions. Linguist John McWhorter's musings about translating Shakespeare is what sparked this project. First published in his 1998 book *Word on the Street* and reprinted in 2010 in *American Theatre* magazine, he notes that the "irony today is that the Russians, the French, and other people in foreign countries possess Shakespeare to a much greater extent than we do, for the simple reason that they get to enjoy Shakespeare in the language they speak."

This intrigued Dave Hitz, a long-time patron of the Oregon Shakespeare Festival, and he offered to support a project that looked at Shakespeare's plays through the lens of the English we speak today. How much has the English language changed since Shakespeare? Is it possible that there are conventions in the early modern English of Shakespeare that don't translate to us today, especially in the moment of hearing it spoken out loud as one does in the theater?

How might we "carry forward" the successful communication between actor and audience that took place 400 years ago? "Carry forward," by the way, is what we mean by "translate." It is the fourth definition of *translate* in the Oxford English Dictionary.

As director of literary development and dramaturgy at the Oregon Shakespeare Festival, I was given the daunting task of figuring out how to administer the project. I began with Kenneth Cavander, who translates ancient Greek tragedies into English. I figured that someone who does that kind of work would lend an air of seriousness to the project. I asked him, how might he go about translating from the source language of early modern English into the target language of contemporary modern English?

He looked at different kinds of speech: rhetorical and poetical, soliloquies and crowd scenes, and the puns in comedies. What emerged from his tinkering became a template for the translation commission. These weren't rules exactly, but instructions that every writer was given.

First, do no harm. There is plenty of the language that doesn't need translating. And there is some that does. Every playwright had different criteria for assessing what to change.

Second, go line-by-line. No editing, no cutting, no "fixing." I want the whole play translated. We often cut the gnarly bits in Shakespeare for performance. What might we make of those bits if we understood them in the moment of hearing them? Might we be less compelled to cut?

Third, all other variables stay the same: the time period, the story, the characters, their motivations, and their thoughts. We designed the experiment to examine the language.

Fourth, and most important, the language must follow the same kind of rigor and pressure as the original, which means honoring the meter, rhyme, rhetoric, image, metaphor, character, action, and theme. Shakespeare's astonishingly compressed language must be respected. Trickiest of all: making sure to work within the structure of the iambic pentameter.

We also didn't know which of Shakespeare's plays might benefit from this kind of investigation: the early comedies, the late tragedies, the highly poetic plays. So we asked three translators who translate plays from other languages into English to examine a Shakespeare play from each genre outlined in the *First Folio*: Kenneth took on *Timon of Athens,* a tragedy; Douglas Langworthy worked on the *Henry the Sixth* history plays, and Ranjit Bolt tried his hand at the comedy *Much Ado about Nothing.*

Kenneth's *Timon* received a production at the Alabama Shakespeare in 2014 and it was on the plane ride home that I thought about expanding the project to include 39 plays. And I wanted to do them all at once. The idea was to capture a snapshot of contemporary modern English. I couldn't oversee that many commissions, and when Ken Hitz (Dave's brother and president of the Hitz Foundation) suggested that we add a dramaturg to each play, the plan suddenly unfolded in front of me. The next day, I made a simple, but extensive, proposal to Dave on how to commission and develop 39 translations in three years. He responded immediately with "Yes."

My initial thought was to only commission translators who translate plays. But I realized that "carry forward" has other meanings. There was a playwright in the middle of the conversation 400 years ago. What would it mean to carry *that* forward?

For one thing, it would mean that we wanted to examine the texts through the lens of performance. I am interested in learning how a dramatist makes sense of the play. Basically, we asked the writers to create performable companion pieces.

I wanted to tease out what we mean by contemporary modern English, and so we created a matrix of writers who embodied many different lived experiences: age, ethnicity, gender-identity, experience with translations, geography, English as a second language, knowledge of Shakespeare, etc.

What the playwrights had in common was a deep love of language and a curiosity about the assignment. Not everyone was on board with the idea and I was eager to see how the experiment would be for them.

They also pledged to finish the commission within three years.

To celebrate the completion of the translations, we produced a festival in June 2019 in partnership with The Classic Stage Company in New York to hear all 39 of them. Four hundred years ago I think we went to *hear* a play; today we often go to *see* a play. In the staged reading format of the Festival, we heard these plays as if for the first time. The blend of Shakespeare with another writer was seamless and jarring at the same time. Countless actors and audience members told us that the plays were understandable in ways they had never been before.

Now it's time to share the work. We were thrilled when Ayanna Thompson and her colleagues at the Arizona Center for Medieval and Renaissance Studies offered to publish the translations for us.

I ask that you think of these as marking a moment in time. The editions published in this series are based on the scripts that were used in the Play on! Festival in 2019. For the purpose of the readings, there were cuts allowed and these scripts represent those reading drafts.

The original commission tasked the playwrights and dramaturg to translate the whole play. The requirement of the commission was for two drafts which is enough to put the ball in play. The real fun with these texts is when there are actors, a director, a dramaturg, and the playwright wrestling with them together in a rehearsal room.

The success of a project of this scale depends on the collaboration and contributions of many people. The playwrights and dramaturgs took the assignment seriously and earnestly and were humble and gracious throughout the development of the translations. SallyCade Holmes and Holmes Productions, our producer since the beginning, provided a steady and calm influence.

We have worked with more than 1,200 artists in the development of these works. We have partnered with more than three dozen theaters and schools. Numerous readings and more than a dozen productions of these translations have been heard and seen in the United States as well as Canada, England, and The Czech Republic.

There is a saying in the theater that 80% of the director's job is taken care of when the production is cast well. Such was my luck when I hired Taylor Bailey, who has overseen every reading and workshop. Our great cast is rounded out with Summer Martin, Kamilah Long, Katie Kennedy, and Jacourtney Mountain-Bluhm.

All of this has come to be because Bill Rauch, then artistic director of the Oregon Shakespeare Festival, said yes when Dave Hitz pitched the idea to him in 2011. Actually he said, "Hmm, interesting," which I translated to "yes." I am dearly indebted to that 'yes.'

My gratitude to Dave, Ken, and the Hitz Foundation can never be fully expressed. Their generosity, patience, and unwavering belief in what we are doing has given us the confidence to follow the advice of Samuel Beckett: "Ever tried. Ever failed. No matter. Try again. Fail again. Fail better."

Play on!

Dr. Lue Douthit
CEO/Creative Director at Play on Shakespeare
October 2020

WHAT WAS I THINKING?

A Journey through the Scottish Highlands
with Shakespeare and *Macbeth*
by Migdalia Cruz

"Everyone will think you're crazy to do such a thing."

The commission to translate one of the most revered texts by one of the most revered playwrights in the White Male Western Canon and help it speak to a 21st Century audience that includes everyone else — was an intellectually rigorous yet delicate journey. In my attempt to clarify *Macbeth* for a modern ear, was it possible to maintain Shakespeare's original intentions, poetry and rhythms, place and characters, without losing myself and the integrity of the work in the process?

I began with two text sources: The First Folio and Arden's 3rd Edition, paying strict attention to the original poetry to maintain the various meters in his text — which were not solely iambic pentameter, but also couplets, blank verse, trochaic tetrameter, and incomplete (catalectic) trochaic tetrameter. Then I investigated every word's meaning and pronunciation, studying scholarly works about semiotics and language — all necessary to understand the play as a whole and respect the enormous inventory of research.

I reviewed the history of both 12th century Scotland and 16th century England, along with the Gunpowder Plot, and the rise of supernatural beliefs in the 1400s to 1500s. I researched every bawdy reference and each curse. I struggled with thou vs. you. And

I constantly asked myself: Do I understand what is being said just by hearing it?

Lue Douthit offered me other plays to translate for the PlayOn! Project @OSF, but I chose *Macbeth*. Family secrets, ambition, the powerless seeking power by any means then facing the consequences — read like a Migdalia Cruz play to me. *Macbeth* is a play about how mourning the loss of a baby, of kingdoms, of country, leads to an inevitable tragedy guided by fate. This is what I write about — mourning. My first essay was about my friend who was raped and murdered at age eight. Writing is how I mourned her. Mourning is *Macbeth*.

Research took me down many roads, but I still needed to internalize Shakespeare's Macbeth so I could deconstruct it in order to re-construct it with my Latinx sensibility and my woman's gaze. I had to add my voice to it and find a reason why I was working on this play at this time in history. I had to understand: who was Macbeth — the man?

When I write, I create altars to my characters, containing talismans, music, colors, and objects — not necessarily something with crosses or any kind of religious symbols — but an assembly of sacred objects that belong to characters, or a time in my life, or a place that is important to the character or to the story. To collect material for my *Macbeth* altar, I travelled to the Isle of Iona in the Hebrides to find his grave and pray for permission to enter his world. In a way, it was also a spiritual journey to my own thoughts on who he was and what he meant to Scotland and to Shakespeare as he wrote about him for James I.

Once I felt I could enter this world, I studied the other characters and felt a kinship with the Witches. What are they and what do I want them to do? To me they are women of color surrounding this world, contextualizing it in order to recreate it. Their power comes from their sexual attraction — alluring and scary — in particular

Isle of Iona in the Hebrides, looking toward Isle of Mull and the High-lands beyond.
Photo Credit: James Kent.

to men who do not want their positions challenged. I didn't want old hags in the forest. That witch idea died decades ago. What does a modern witch look like? What do powerful women look like? Or women who understand fate and destiny? The Witches hover over the story, commenting and shaping the future, ushering us into the 21st century. They sing soul songs in the style of girl groups from the 1960s, bringing some of my sensibility to the work.

In contextualizing the play through them, I added words for them, just as Shakespeare, or his editors, also added words for them in their songs taken from Thomas Middleton. I thought: 'if he's stealing from other people, he might as well steal from Cruz,' so I added intros to scenes, songs, etc., making it sound more like a play of mine. From there I began to re-construct the play as I understood it. This was my visceral way into this world — where everyone fears the women who tell the truth about the future. I recognize this journey as my own. We live in a time when a Black

Trinidad Ramkissoon, Jade Guerra, Alex Casillas as The Witches from Actors' Shakespeare Project of Boston's production of Macbeth (translated by M. Cruz), November 2018.
Photo Credit: Nile Scott Shots

student napping on a dormitory couch can elicit a call to 911. What are we most afraid of in the 21st Century United States?

Doing harm to a White man who's been dead for over 400 Years?

To test and push the language, I worked with the brilliant actress/dramaturg, Ishia Bennison who brought to the process her experience of performing and teaching Shakespeare with the RSC, and her former company, Northern Broadsides. We performed a word-by-word analysis and clarification — sometimes as fast as one sentence per hour. We combed through the script. She read aloud with all her RSC cred. I brought my Bronx-bred *coraje* and put the play together in a way in which we both understood all the words, the context and the poetry. Together we re-imagined words, syntax, placement, and tried our best to keep the best of Shakespeare intact without sacrificing the originality of Migdalia. Ishia, as an actress, also helped me double-check that the words said aloud were speakable for American and British actors.

So far, I have been blessed with two productions of *Macbeth*. Dealing with a living playwright was a tough sell to many Shakespeare companies, when they can cut Shakespeare to shreds and not pay royalties. Two brave companies stepped up: Actors' Shakespeare Project in Boston and the African-American Shakespeare Company in San Francisco. Both productions were rich and clear. They both used actors of color — for major characters — not just sword-bearers and servants. Both companies addressed my greatest wish, that this play — as with all my plays — be performed by actors of color. I wanted to create works that resonate for audiences who may have felt left out of the Shakespeare canon in the past, except in minor roles written to make them sound like White upper-class British people. A language and a text for all people — that was my goal.

This "crazy 'translation' thing" made me appreciate how another writer's words and stories deepen your understanding of your own work. The act of disassembling and then rebuilding strengthens your craft. And how delicious, as a Puerto Rican woman from the Bronx, to become part of the Western Canon in this subversive way! People of color are clearly entitled to these classic works, and, in a deeper way, entitled to poetry without question, explanation or rancor. That's what I was thinking.

I thank Lue Douthit of OSF's PlayOn! Project for placing me on such an invigorating path and to the Hitz Foundation for supporting it.

Migdalia Cruz
July 2020

CAST OF CHARACTERS

{brackets} denote pronunciation

The Three WITCHES

DUNCAN, King of Scotland

MALCOLM, elder son of Duncan

A Sergeant/CAPTAIN

LENNOX, nobleman of Scotland

ROSS, nobleman of Scotland

MACBETH, Thane of Glamis *{Glarms}* and Cawdor *{Cordoor}*, a general in the King's army

BANQUO, Thane of Lochaber, a general in the King's army

ANGUS, nobleman of Scotland

LADY MACBETH, his wife

FLEANCE, Banquo's son

A PORTER

MACDUFF, Thane of Fife, a nobleman of Scotland

DONALBAIN, younger son of Duncan

An OLD MAN

The Three MURDERERS

HECATE, Queen of the Witches

The APPARITIONS

LADY MACDUFF, Macduff's wife

Boy, Son of MACDUFF

A Scottish DOCTOR

GENTLEWOMAN attending on Lady Macbeth

MENTEITH, nobleman of Scotland

CAITHNESS, nobleman of Scotland

SEYTON, attendant to Macbeth

SIWARD, Earl of Northumberland, general of the English forces
YOUNG SIWARD, his son
The Ghost of **BANQUO** (non-speaking role)
LORDS, Gentlemen, Officers, Soldiers, Attendants, Servants, and
    Messengers

PRONUNCIATIONS
In the text, *{bracket}* notes pronunciation of previous word.

Scone = *{Skoon}*   Forres = *{For-Rez}*
Glamis = *{Glarms}*   Sweno = *{Swee-no}*
Cawdor = *{Cordoor}*   Birnam = *{Burr-nam}*
Colmekill = *{Coomekill}*   Dunsinane = *{Done-see-nayne}*
Nonpareil = *{Nonparay}*   Acheron = *{Ackeron}*
Hecate = *{Heck-eight}*   Siward = *{See-word}*

ACT 1 ◆ SCENE 1

A BARREN, WAR-TORN LANDSCAPE

Thunder and lightning usher in three Witches

ALL *(from the darkness)*

When will we three make a King?

Now the storm outside comes in.

Scotland's son's rising as it sets.

What one gives is what one gets.

WITCH 1

When will we three meet again?   5

In Thunder, lightning, or in rain?

WITCH 2

When the hurlyburly's done,

When the battle's lost and won.

WITCH 3

Before the setting of the Sun.

WITCH 1   Where the place?

WITCH 2

Upon the heath.

WITCH 3   There to meet with Macbeth.   10

Witch 1's familiar sounds a plaintive meow

WITCH 1

I come, Graymalkin!

Witch 2's familiar sounds a toad's croak

WITCH 2   Paddock calls.

WITCH 3   Soon then!

ALL

Fair is foul, and foul is fair:

Hover through the fog and filthy air.

Exit

1

ACT 1 ◆ SCENE 2

A BATTLE ENCAMPMENT NEAR FORRES

A call to arms within

Enter King Duncan, Malcolm, Lennox, with attendants,
meeting a bleeding Captain

DUNCAN

Who is this bloody man? He can report —
By the looks of him, all the latest news
Of the revolt.

MALCOLM

This is the Sergeant,
Who like a good and hardy soldier, fought   5
Gainst my captivity — Hail, brave friend!
Say to the King your knowledge of the battle
As you last left it.

CAPTAIN   Doubtful it stood;
Like two spent swimmers that do cling together
Stealing each other's breath. The merciless Macdonald,   10
A worthy enemy this rebel,
Whose Villainous Nature draws
Men to follow him, from the Irish Isles
Brought mercenaries and his own axe-men
Making Fickle Fortune smile on his damned death-pile   15
like a Rebel's whore — but t'was too weak
For Brave Macbeth, well he deserves that name,
Disdaining Fortune, with his brandished Sword
Which still burned with bloody execution —
Like Valour's servant, carved out his passage   20
Until he faced that swine,
But never shook hands, nor wished him farewell,
Just ripped him open from entrails to entrance,
And rammed his head atop our battlements.

DUNCAN

O valiant cousin! Worthy gentleman!   25

CAPTAIN

And from the East where the loyal Sun rises,

Shipwrecking storms and fearful thunders break,

So from that spring, where comfort seemed to come

Discomfort rises: mark, King of Scotland, mark:

No sooner had justice, armed with valour,   30

Compelled these paid soldiers to turn their heels,

But, Sweno *{Swee-no}*, the Norwegian King, sensing advantage,

With replenished weapons and new supplies of men

Began a fresh assault.

DUNCAN

Did this not dismay our Captains Macbeth and Banquo?   35

CAPTAIN

Yes; as Sparrows are dismayed by eagles or hares by lions:

In truth, I must report they were

Like overcharged cannons with double the ammunition.

They doubly redoubled their efforts against the enemy:

Unless they meant to swim in their gushing wounds,   40

Or re-enact another Crucifixion hill,

I couldn't say — but I am faint;

My gashes cry for help.

DUNCAN

Your words as well as your wounds show courage:

They smack of honour both. Go, get him surgeons.   45

Exit Captain with attendants. Enter Ross and Angus

Who comes here?

MALCOLM   The worthy Thane of Ross.

LENNOX

What a frantic look in his eyes!

So look those who speak of frightful things.

3

ROSS

God save the King.

DUNCAN

Where cam'st from, worthy Ross?

ROSS   From Fife, great King.   50

Where the Norwegian banners scornfully fly

And fan our people cold.

Norway's king — with terrifying numbers,

Assisted by that most disloyal traitor —

Macdonald, the Thane of Cawdor *{Cordoor}*, began a deadly

conflict;   55

Brave Macbeth, clad in impenetrable armour,

Point against point, rebellious arm 'gainst arm,

Ravished his unholy spirit and finally,

The Victory fell on us.

DUNCAN   Great Happiness!

ROSS

And now Sweno *{Swee-know}*, the Norwegian King,   60

Craves complete accord:

Nor would we let him bury his men

At Saint Columba's Isle, until he paid

Ten thousand dollars *{dough-lars}*, for our general use.

DUNCAN

No more will that Thane of Cawdor *{Cordoor}* destroy   65

Our deep interests. Pronounce his impending death,

And with his former title, now greet Macbeth.

ROSS

I'll see it's done.

DUNCAN

What he has lost, noble Macbeth has won.

Exit

ACT 1 ◆ SCENE 3

A HEATH

The sound of thunder. The Three Witches enter

WITCH 1

Where have you been, Sister?

WITCH 2

Killing swine.

WITCH 3 *(meaning Witch 1)*

Sister, and you?

WITCH 1

A Sailor's wife had chestnuts in her lap,

And munched and munched and munched: 5

'Give me,' said I —

"Begone, witch!" the swill-fed swinelet cries.

Her husband's sailed to Aleppo, Captain of the Tiger:

But in a sieve, I'll follow his sail,

And like a horny rat without a tail, 10

I'll do, I'll do, I'll do him.

WITCH 2

I'll give you a wind. *{Rhyme with "kind"}*

WITCH 1

How kind.

WITCH 3

And I another.

WITCH 1

I myself have all the other; 15

Fanned the very ports they blow,

And all the places that they know

From their sailing chart.

I'll drain him dry as hay:

Sleep won't come in Night or Day 20

To hang upon his swollen lids;

5

Cursed, he'll live a man forbid.

Not sleeping for nine weeks times nine —

He'll dwindle, peak and then he'll pine:

Though his boat will not be lost, 25

Still it will be tempest-tossed.

Look what I have!

WITCH 2

Show me, show me!

WITCH 1

Here I have a Captain's thumb,

Wrecked as homeward, he did come. 30

We hear the sound of a drum

WITCH 3

A drum! A drum!

Macbeth does come.

ALL

Come Weïrd Sisters — hand in hand,

Travelers over sea and land —

Let us spin about, about: 35

Three to you, three to me,

And thrice more times toward destiny.

Peace! The spell is spun.

Macbeth and Banquo enter

MACBETH

I have not seen a day so fair and foul.

BANQUO

How much further to Forres? *{For-Rez}* What are these, 40

So withered and so wild in their attire,

They look not like they walk the Earth,

And yet are on it? Alive? Or are you something

That man may not question? You seem to understand me

Since you've placed a boney finger 45

6

Upon your skinny lips: you should be women,
And yet your beards forbid me from taking
You for fair ones.

MACBETH

Speak, if you can: What are you?

WITCH 1

All hail, Macbeth! Hail to thee, Thane of Glamis! *{Glarms}*   50

WITCH 2

All hail, Macbeth! Hail to you, Thane of Cawdor! *{Cordoor}*

WITCH 3

Hey, ho, Macbeth! That shall be King soon after.

BANQUO *(to Macbeth)*

Good Sir, why do you jump and fear
Things that sound so fair?

(to the Witches)

Tell me true —   55
Are you an illusion? Or that indeed
Which you outwardly show? Gracefully you greet
My noble partner, with great predictions,
Of lordly laurels and royal promise,
That he is by you enrapt: but to me no words.   60
If you can look into the seeds of time,
And say which grain will grow, and which will not,
Speak then to me, who neither begs nor fears
Your favors nor your hate.

WITCH 1

Hail!   65

WITCH 2

Hail!

WITCH 3

Hey!

WITCH 1

Lesser than Macbeth, but greater.

WITCH 2

Not so happy, yet much happier.

WITCH 3

You'll beget kings but never get a crown.   70

So all hail, Macbeth and Banquo!

WITCH 1 & 2

Banquo and Macbeth, all hail!

MACBETH

Stay, you imperfect speakers! Tell me more.

I was Thane of Glamis *{Glarms}* upon my father's death

But how Thane of Cawdor *{Cordoor}*, if that Thane still lives?   75

A prosperous gentleman: And to be King

Simply quite impossible to believe,

No more than to be Cawdor *{Cordoor}*. From where

Did you gather such strange information? Why

On this bloody Heath do you transfix us   80

With your damn prophecies?! Speak! I say.

Witches vanish

BANQUO

The earth has bubbles, as does the water,

Just like these creatures. To where have they vanished?

MACBETH

Into the Air; What seemed so solid,

Melted as breath, into the wind.   85

Wish they had stayed!

BANQUO

Were they really here, those we speak about?

Or have we drunk an insane elixir

That takes our reason prisoner?

MACBETH

  Your children shall be kings.   90

BANQUO

  You will be King.

MACBETH

  And Thane of Cawdor *{Cordoor}* too: didn't they say?

BANQUO

  That's the song they sang us — Who's there?

                Ross and Angus enter

ROSS

  The King has happily received, Macbeth,

  The news of your success: and when he heard   95

  Of your part in this victory 'gainst the rebels,

  He could not separate his great triumph

  From your own valour; which gave him grateful pause.

  Then he discovered on that self-same day,

  You led another defense against the Norwegian Army   100

  Where, unafraid of Death, and as its agent, a massacre

  You left in your wake. As thick as hail

  Fell man after man and message after message,

  Where all rang Macbeth's praises in this Kingdom's great defense

  And sang them down before him.

ANGUS   We are sent,   105

  To give you thanks from our Royal master;

  By ushering you into his sight

  Not pay you.

ROSS

  And, in promise of a greater honour

  From him, he bid me call you Thane of Cawdor: *{Cordoor}*   110

  So by this new title, Hail, most worthy Thane,

  For it is yours.

BANQUO   What, can those Devils speak true?!

MACBETH

    The Thane of Cawdor *{Cordoor}* lives:

    Why do you dress me in borrowed robes?

ANGUS   Who was the Thane, still lives;

    But he is under judgment for his life,   115

    Which he deserves to lose.

    Whether he was aligned with the Norwegians,

    Or did offer the Rebels hidden help

    Or advantage, or if with both he worked

    To wreck his own country, I know not,   120

    But his treason, a capital offense,

    Has already been confessed and proved,

    And have overthrown him.

MACBETH *(an aside)*

    Glamis *{Glarms}*, and Thane of Cawdor *{Cordoor}*:

    The greatest is yet to come.   125

(to Ross and Angus)

    Thanks for your pains.

(to Banquo)

    Do you not hope your children will be Kings

    When those that gave me Thane of Cawdor

    Promised them the throne?

BANQUO   That, trusted fully,

    Might yet light your way to the Crown   130

    Now that you are Cawdor — but at what price?

    It is strange how often that to lead us

    Into dire harm, the Dark Devils and Demons tell us truths,

    Fool us with honest trifles, to betray us

    With deepest consequence.   135

(to Angus and Ross)

    Cousins, a word, I pray you.

MACBETH *(aside)*   Two truths are told,

As happy prologues to the rising act
With royal themes. — I thank you, gentlemen. —
All these supernatural predictions
Cannot be bad, cannot be good. If bad,   140
Why did it give me a taste of success,
By starting with the truth? I am Thane of Cawdor: *{Cordoor}*
If good, why succumb to a suggestion
So horrid that my hair does stand on end
And makes my steady heart knock at my ribs,   145
Against the beat of Nature? My fears filled
With horrible imaginings. My thoughts
Of murder, yet unrealized, do now
Shake my belief in myself, smothering
My unborn actions with torturous thoughts   150
And nothing is, but what is not.

BANQUO

Look, our partner's entranced.

MACBETH *(aside)*

If Chance will make me King,
why Chance may crown me,
Without my help.

BANQUO   Honours fall upon him,   155
Like new garments only mould to the form
Aided by use, o'er time.

MACBETH *(aside)*   Come what come may,
Time moves on even through the roughest day.

BANQUO

Worthy Macbeth, we are waiting to serve you.

MACBETH

You must forgive me: 160
My dull brain was full of things forgotten.
Kind gentlemen, your efforts are inscribed

Where each day, I'll see them and remember.

Let us go now to the King.

(to Banquo)

Think on what has happened and when we've time,   165

after weighing it all, let's speak freely

our hearts to each other.

BANQUO   Very gladly.

MACBETH

Till then, enough: Come, friends.

Exit

ACT 1 ◆ SCENE 4

IN FORRES *{FOR-REZ}*. A ROOM IN DUNCAN'S PALACE

We hear a flourish of trumpets

Duncan, Malcolm, Donalbain, Lennox, and Attendants enter

DUNCAN

Has Cawdor *{Cordoor}* been executed? Have those

Fulfilling that duty not returned?

MALCOLM   My Liege,

They have not as yet come back; but I spoke

To one who saw him die: who reported

That he openly confessed his treasons,   5

Begged your highness' pardon, and offered

A deep repentance. Nothing in his life

Became him like the leaving of it: he died

As one who is practiced in his own dying,

Throwing away the dearest thing owned,   10

As if it had no meaning.

DUNCAN   There's no art

To know a man's mind from seeing his face:

He was a gentleman on whom I built

An absolute trust.

Macbeth, Banquo, Ross, and Angus enter
Oh, worthiest cousin!
The sin of my ingratitude even now   15
Weighs heavy on me. You are so worthy
Of a swift reward for your loyalty,
But it's slow to come. Had you deserved less,
I could repay you in thanks and coin!
I have only one thing left to say: 20
Your worth is more than all I can pay.

MACBETH
The service and the loyalty I owe,
Pays for itself in doing so.
Your Highness' role is to receive our duties:
And our duties are to your throne, and state.   25
As children & servants, we do all we must
To protect your Love and Honour,
And to keep your trust.

DUNCAN   Welcome home now:
I have planted you firmly in my soil and will nourish
You, till you bloom and flourish. Noble Banquo,   30
Let no one say that you deserve any less,
For all you have done — let me embrace you.
And place you near my heart.

BANQUO   If I grow there
The harvest is yours, Sire.

DUNCAN   My abundant joys,
Shamefully full, try to hide themselves   35
In Sorrow's tears. Sons, Kinsmen, Thanes,
And you who are my nearest allies, know
We will name as our most worthy heir:
Malcolm, our eldest, whom we now will call
The Prince of Cumberland: May this Noble honour,   40

13

Be as a star and brightly shine on all those worthy.

Now let's press to Inverness,

To bind us further to you.

MACBETH

Leave the rest to me —

I'll be the messenger and make joyful   45

My wife upon hearing of your approach;

So, humbly, I take my leave.

DUNCAN   My worthy Cawdor! *{Cordoor}*

MACBETH *(aside)*

The Prince of Cumberland! He is a step

On which I must stumble, or otherwise leap,

Right in my way it lies. Stars snuff out your light!   50

Do not shine on my dark and deep desires.

The eye winks at the Hand; but now let it see

That what the eye fears is what has to be.

Macbeth exits

DUNCAN

True, worthy Banquo: Macbeth's so fully valiant,

That by praising him I am fed;   55

He is a banquet to me. Let's follow him,

To where he's gone to bid us welcome:

He is a peerless kinsman.

A flourish of trumpets. Exit

ACT 1 ◆ SCENE 5

A ROOM IN MACBETH'S CASTLE AT INVERNESS

Lady Macbeth enters reading a letter from Macbeth

LADY MACBETH

"*They met me on the day of our Success:*

and I have learned from their perfect predictions

they have more than mere mortal knowledge.

14

When I was burning with desire to question them further,
they made themselves Air into which they vanished.   5
As I stood rapt in wonder, messengers from the King
arrived and all hailed me "Thane of Cawdor," {Cordoor}
just as those Weïrd Sisters had, before saluting
me with "Hail, King that shall Be!" —
predicting what only time would determine.   10
This I share with you, my dearest partner in greatness,
so you do not miss a moment of rejoicing
in the greatness promised to you.
Keep this secret close to your heart and farewell."
Glamis {Glarms} you are, and Cawdor; and shall be   15
What you've been promised: but I fear your nature
Too full of the milk of human kindness
To do what you must. You would be great;
And do not lack ambition, but may lack
The ruthlessness to further it.   20
What is your right, you want to rightly win:
And never would you do the unholy thing,
And yet would by any means win.
You have to do, great Glamis {Glarms}, what now cries
To be done, to have what you desire.   25
Men do what they most fear to do,
even if they will wish it undone.
Hurry home, husband,
So I may pour my spirits in your ear,
And melt your doubts with my courageous tongue;   30
Doubts that stop you from pursuit of the Crown,
When fate and mystical forecasts do seem
To have already made you King.

A Messenger enters

                                        What news do you bring?

MESSENGER

The King comes here tonight.

LADY MACBETH   You must be mad!

Is not your master with him? If he were   35

He would have warned me to prepare.

MESSENGER

Please, my lady, it is true: our Thane is coming.

Another messenger rode ahead of him,

Who, with almost his last breath,

Gave me this message for you.

LADY MACBETH   Take care of him: 40

He brings great news.

Messenger exits. We hear the call of a Raven

The Raven himself is hoarse

That croaks the fatal entrance of Duncan

Under my battlements. Come, you Spirits,

That tend on mortal thoughts, unsex me here,

And fill me from head to toe to top — full   45

Of direst cruelty! Make thick my blood,

Stop its flow and close the passage to regret,

So no remorseful visits of Nature

Shake my savage purpose, nor keeps me from

What I must do! Come to my woman's breasts,   50

And drink my milk for bitter courage,

You murdering ministers! Come, from that place

You formless fiends await Nature's mischief.

Come thick night, and screen your form in the darkest

Smoke of Hell, so my sharp knife sees not   55

The wound it makes, nor Heaven peep through the

Blanket of the dark to cry, "Hold, Hold."

Macbeth enters

Great Glamis *{Glarms}*, Worthy Cawdor *{Cordoor}*,

Greater than both, by the All Hail-Hereafter!
Your letter transported me beyond   60
This ignorant present, so now I feel
The future in this instant.

MACBETH   My dearest Love,
Duncan comes here to-night.

LADY MACBETH   And when goes hence?

MACBETH
Tomorrow, he proposes.

LADY MACBETH   Oh never
Will he see tomorrow's Sun.   65
Your face, my Thane, is like a book, where men
May read strange matters. To beguile the time,
Act like the time; bear welcome in your eye,
Your hand, your tongue: look like the innocent flower,
But be the serpent under it. He that's coming   70
Must be provided for: so you just leave
The Night's great business in my willing hands;
Which will give all our nights and days to come,
Complete control and dominion.

MACBETH
We will speak further.

LADY MACBETH   Keep your face clear;   75
To change expression is to show fear.
Leave all the rest to me.

Exit

17

ACT 1 ◆ SCENE 6

INVERNESS. IN FRONT OF MACBETH'S CASTLE

We hear the sound of oboes. See the glow of torches
Duncan, Malcolm, Donalbain, Banquo, Lennox, Macduff, Ross,
Angus, and Attendants enter

DUNCAN

This castle is pleasantly placed, the air
Quickly and sweetly invites oneself
To calm the senses.

BANQUO

The guests of summer,
These purple temple-haunting little birds,   5
Show their love for this home, in Heaven's breath,
A smell that woos them here. Each jutting frieze,
Buttress, or corner crevice, has been made
Into a nest and cradle for its young:
Here, where they breed and live, I have observed   10
That the air's delicious.

Lady Macbeth enters

DUNCAN   See, here's our honoured hostess —

The love bestowed us has caused you trouble
For which we thank you with love.
We will offer thanks to God for your pains,
And thank you for your trouble.

LADY MACBETH   All our service,   15

Even if twice done, and then done double,
Could not be equal service, when compared
To all those honours, deep and broad, with which
Your Majesty fills our house: for the past
And the present dignities bestowed us,   20
We owe you prayers.

DUNCAN

    Where's the Thane of Cawdor? *{Cordoor}*

    We raced close behind him, with the sole purpose

    Of helping with this evening's preparations,

    but he rides well;   25

    And, his love of you, sharp as a spur, helped him

    Arrive home before us: Fair and Noble hostess,

    We are your guest tonight.

LADY MACBETH

    Ever your servants,

    We make ourselves, along with our accounts,   30

    Available for your Highness' pleasure —

    To use as your own.

DUNCAN

    Give me your hand;

    Take me to your host: we love him dearly,

    And will extend our praise to him.   35

    If you please, Hostess.

Exit

ACT 1 ◆ SCENE 7

A ROOM IN MACBETH'S CASTLE

Oboes play. Torches burn. Servants, carrying dishes and silverware,
enter and cross the room. Then Macbeth enters

MACBETH

    If it were done, when 'tis done, then 'twere well

    It were done quickly: if the assassination

    Could rein in the consequence, and seize

    With his "ceasing" — success; but that this blow

    Might be the be-all and the end-all, here,   5

    Then here, from this shore to shallow of time,

    We'd jump o'er the life to come. In these cases

We still must be judged; And so we teach
Bloody lessons here, which once taught, return
To haunt the teacher. Even-handed Justice   10
Moves th'ingredient from our poisoned chalice
To our own lips. He's here in double trust:
Firstly, I am his kinsman and his subject,
Strong cause not to kill: Then, as his Host,
Should shield my guests from murderers at my door,   15
Not bear the knife myself. Besides, this Duncan
Has borne his King's power humbly, has been
So fair in his great office, that his virtues
Will plead like angels, trumpet-tongued, against
The deep damnation of his being offed;   20
And pity, like a naked newborn babe
Bursting into life, or Heaven's cherubims,
Soaring upon the unseen couriers of the air,
Will blow the horrid deed in every eye,
That tears will drown the wind. I have no spur   25
To prick the sides of my intent, but only
Vaulting ambition, which jumps over itself
And falls on th'other —

Lady Macbeth enters
now! What news?

LADY MACBETH
He's near done supping. Why did you leave the table?
MACBETH
Has he asked for me?
LADY MACBETH   Of course he has!   30
MACBETH
We will proceed no further in this business:
He has honoured me of late; and I've gained
Glowing opinions from all sorts of people,

And these I'll wear now; my newest garments,
Not cast aside so soon.

LADY MACBETH   Are your hopes drunk,   35
With which you dressed yourself?
Have they slept since?
And wake right now, looking so green and pale,
Made sick by what they once longed for freely?
From now on I will question your love.   40
Can you be as fierce in action and valour
As you are in desire? Would you have what
You esteemed as the crowning glory of life,
Or live a coward in your own esteem,
Letting 'I dare not' come before 'I will,'   45
Like a fish-loving cat who dare not wet its feet?

MACBETH   Pray, peace!
I dare do all that does befit a man —
Who dares do more is none.

LADY MACBETH   What beast was it then,
That made you break to me this venture?
When you dared do it, then you were a man;   50
But to be much more than you were, only Doing
Makes a better man. Not time, nor place,
Seemed quite so right, but now you've made them both:
They are ready now, now that readiness
Does unmake you. I have suckled babes, know   55
How tender 'tis to love the babe that milks me:
But while it was smiling in my face, I'd
Have plucked my nipple from his boneless gums,
And bashed his brains out, had I so sworn
As you have done to this.

MACBETH   If we should fail?   60

LADY MACBETH

We fail.

But screw your courage to the sticking-place,

And we'll not fail. When Duncan is asleep

Brought on quickly as his day's long journey

Soundly invites, his two chamber-men,   65

With wine and wassail I will so convince,

That memory, the warden of the brain,

Will be fumes, and the receipt of all reason

Only a trickle: When in swinish sleep,

Their wine-drenched souls lie, as if in death,   70

What cannot you and I perform upon

The unguarded Duncan? And then cast blame

On his drink-soaked officers, "wearing"

The guilt of our great kill?

MACBETH   Bring forth men-children only!

For your unflinching spirit should conceive   75

Nothing but males. Will it not be received,

Once we have marked with blood those two sleepy

Chamber-men, and used their very own daggers

That they have done it?

LADY MACBETH   Who dares receive otherwise.

As we will make our grief and outcries roar   80

Upon his death?!

MACBETH   I am resolved and offer every bit

Of my body to this terrible feat.

Go now, and mock this time with a sweet show:

False face must hide what the false heart does know.

Blackout; A series of lightning strikes catch the Witches in their light

as if they are in a strobe. The Witches play in the darkness.

WITCHES 1, 2 & 3

Our Brave Macbeth's begun the flood —   85

The water's rising thick with blood.
His lady drags him to its stream —
No one stops her, someone screams.

ACT 2 ♦ SCENE 1

INVERNESS. THE COURT WITHIN MACBETH'S CASTLE

Banquo & his son, Fleance, enter, holding a lit torch

BANQUO

What is the time, boy?

FLEANCE

The moon has set; I have not heard the clock.

BANQUO

And she goes down at twelve.

FLEANCE   I take it, 'tis later, Sir.

BANQUO

Here, take my sword. Heaven is thrifty to-night,

Its candles all burnt out. *(Referring to his dagger)* Take thee this

    too.   5

A heavy summons lies like lead upon me,

And yet I cannot sleep. Merciful Angels!

Keep away the cursed thoughts that plague me in my sleep.

Macbeth and a Servant enter with a lit torch

Give me my sword: Who's there?

MACBETH

A friend.   10

BANQUO

What, Sir! Not yet asleep? The King's in bed:

He has been unusually joyful.

And sent great gifts for your household.

With this diamond, he greets your wife

Such a kind hostess, granting   15

His boundless gratitude.

MACBETH   Being unprepared,

Our welcome was subject to shortcomings
Without which would have served him better.

BANQUO   All's well.

Fleance exits

Last night I dreamt of the three Weïrd Sisters:
They have showed to you some truth.

MACBETH   I think not of them,   20

But when we can uncover an hour to spare,
We could speak some words upon this business
If you would grant the time.

BANQUO   Any time that pleases you.

MACBETH

If you will bring honour to my opinion,
It shall bring honour to you.

BANQUO   So I lose none   25

In seeking to increase it, and still keep
My heart true and free and my loyalty clear,
I will listen to you.

MACBETH   Meanwhile sleep well.

BANQUO

Thanks, Sir. The like to you.

Banquo exits

MACBETH *(to the Servant)*

Go, bid thy mistress when my night-cap's ready   30
She strike upon the bell. Get thee to bed.

Servant exits. Macbeth catches sight of something

Is this a dagger which I see before me,
The handle toward my hand? Come, let me clutch thee.
I have thee not, and yet I see thee still.
Fatal vision, art thou not meant to be   35
Held as firmly as seen? Or art thou but
A dagger of the mind, a false creation,

26

Conjured by a feverish enflamed brain?
Still, I see thee, seeming as deadly real
As this *(pulling out a real dagger)* which now I draw.   40
Thou ushers me further down that fatal path;
The self-same instrument I was to use.
Do'th' other senses make mine eyes foolish
Or are they wiser than the rest? I still see thee;
And on thy blade, and thy hilt, drops of blood,   45
Which was not so before. There's no such thing.
It is the bloody business bidding
This vision to mine eyes. Now o'er half the world
Sleeps as sound as the Dead, nightmares poison
That curtained sleep: Foul Witchcraft honours   50
Moon-pale Hecate — offers Old Man Murder,
warned by his watchman the wolf,
Whose howl speeds him with a stealthy pace,
And a rapist's stride, to his ravished goal
In ghostly silence. Thou sure and firm-set earth,   55
Hear not my steps, which way they walk, for fear
Thy stones will whisper of my where-abouts,
And take away the horror of surprise
Which suits the time. While I speak, he lives;
Words blown cold cool the heat the deed gives.   60
                A bell rings
I go, and it is done: the bell invites me.
Hear it not, Duncan; for its death knell
Will summon thee to Heaven or to Hell.
                Macbeth exits

ACT 2 ◆ SCENE 2
A CHAMBER IN MACBETH'S CASTLE
Lady Macbeth enters

LADY MACBETH

The wine that made them drunk has made me bold:
What has quenched them has lit me on fire.

The sound of an owl

Hark! Peace. It was the owl that shrieked,
A fatal bellman, which gives the final goodnight.
He is about it. The doors are open,   5
and the gluttonous grooms shirk their duties
with snores. I have drugged their drinks,
So now Death and Nature battle o'er them,
Whether they live, or die.

MACBETH *(from offstage)*

              Who's there? What's that!

LADY MACBETH

Oh no I am afraid they have awakened,   10
And 'tis not done. The attempt, and not the deed
Confounds us. Listen! I laid their daggers ready;
He could not miss them. Had Duncan not resembled
My father as he slept, I had done it.

Enter Macbeth

My husband?   15

MACBETH

I have done the deed.
Did you hear nothing?

LADY MACBETH

I heard the owl scream, and the crickets cry.
Did you not speak?

MACBETH   When?

LADY MACBETH   Now.

MACBETH   As I descended?

LADY MACBETH

  Ay.   20

MACBETH

  Listen, who lies in the second chamber?

LADY MACBETH

  Donalbain.

MACBETH *(looking at his hands)*

  This is a sorry sight.

LADY MACBETH

  A foolish thought to say a sorry sight.

MACBETH

  One groom did laugh in his sleep,   25

  As the other cried, "Murder!" so waking each other.

  I stayed and listened; but they just said their prayers

  And lulled themselves back to sleep.

LADY MACBETH

  They are both lodged together.

MACBETH

  One cried, "God bless us!" and, "Amen," the other,   30

  When they saw my bloody hangman's hands.

  Hearing their fear, I could not say, "Amen,"

  When they did say, "God bless us."

LADY MACBETH

  Do not dwell on it so deeply.

MACBETH

  But why could I not pronounce "Amen"?   35

  I needed a true blessing, but "Amen"

  Stuck in my throat.

LADY MACBETH   You must not think these thoughts —

  If you do, these deeds will make us mad.

MACBETH

Methought, I heard a voice cry, "Sleep no more!
Macbeth does murder Sleep," — the innocent Sleep,   40
Sleep, that knits back together our unraveled cares,
That brings death to each day, work's soothing bath,
A balm for our troubled minds, great Nature's
Main course, nourishing life's feast.

LADY MACBETH   What do you mean?

MACBETH

Still it cried, "Sleep no more!" throughout the house: 45
"Glamis *{Glarms}* hath murdered Sleep, and therefore Cawdor
    {Cordoor}
Shall sleep no more, Macbeth will sleep no more!"

LADY MACBETH

Who was it that thus cried? My worthy Thane,
You do deform your noble strength, to think
Of such brainsickly things. Go, get some water   50
To wash this filthy witness from your hand.

Noticing that he still holds the daggers

And why did you bring these daggers from the place?
They must stay there. Go, carry them, and smear
The sleeping grooms with blood.

MACBETH   I'll go no more:

I'm afraid to think of what I have done;   55
Look on it again I dare not.

LADY MACBETH   Men are weak.

Give me the daggers. The sleeping and the dead
Are as harmless as pictures; only the eye of a child
Fears a painted devil. If he still bleeds,
I'll gild red-gold the faces of the grooms,   60
For it must show their guilt.

Lady Macbeth exits. Knocking offstage

MACBETH   From where's that knocking?
  What's wrong with me, when every noise appalls me?
  Whose hands are these? Ha! They pluck out mine eyes.
  Will all great Neptune's ocean wash this blood
  Clean from my hands? No, my hands will so stain   65
  The deep and infinite seas incarnadine,
  Making the green — one red.

Lady Macbeth reenters

LADY MACBETH
  My hands are stained like yours; but it'd shame me
  To have a heart so white with fear.

Knock at the Castle gate

  I hear a knocking at the south entry.   70
  Let us retire to our chamber.
  A little water washes us of this deed.
  How easy it was then! Your disarming fear
  Has left you unguarded.

More knocking

               Hark! More knocking.
  Get on your night-clothes, lest someone greet us,   75
  And prove us to be sleepless night-watchmen.
  Be not lost in pain-filled thoughts.

MACBETH
  To know my deed, 'twere best not know myself.

Knock

  Wake Duncan with thy knocking? I wish thou couldst.

Exit

31

ACT 2 ◆ SCENE 3
OUTSIDE THE SOUTH GATE OF MACBETH'S CASTLE

A Porter enters

Knocking from offstage

PORTER

There's a knocking, indeed! If a man were porter of Hell Gate, he should have plenty of key-turning to do here.

Knocking

Knock, knock, knock. Who i'th'name of Beelzebub is there? Here's a greedy farmer, who tripled his prices, then hanged himself when the grain became cheap: come in, Father Time; have   5
hankerchiefs about you for here you'll sweat like hell.

Knocking

Knock, knock. Who's there, i'th'devil's other name? Faith, here's a lawyer, who could swear against the scales of justice on either side who lied enough for God's sake, yet could not lie to God: O! come in, Father Equivocator.   10

Knocking

Knock, knock, knock. Who's there? Faith, here's a dodgey English tail-or come hither for stealing the crotch from a French panty: come in, tailor; here you may cook your carrot.

Knocking

Knock, knock. Never stays quiet! What are you? But this place is too cold for Hell. I'll devil-porter it no more: I had   15
thought to have let in some from all professions, that go down the primrose path to th'Devil's everlasting bone-fire.

Knocking

Anon, anon: Let me … come!

Holding out a hand for a tip as He opens the gate for Macduff

and Lennox

I pray you, remember the Porter.

Enter Macduff and Lennox

MACDUFF

Was it so late, friend, 'fore you went to bed,   20

That you do de-lay so long?

PORTER

Faith, Sir, we were carousing till the second cock…crows;

and drink, Sir, is a great provoker of three things.

MACDUFF

What three things does drink especially provoke?

PORTER

O, why, Sir, bright-red nose-painting, deep sleep, and urine.   25

Now lechery, Sir, it provokes, and un-provokes: it provokes the

desire, but it takes away the performance. Therefore, much

drink may be said to be an equivocator with lechery: it makes

him, and it mars him; it sets him on, and it takes him off;

it persuades him, and disheartens him; makes him stand to, and   30

not stand to: in conclusion, equivocates him into laying, and,

giving him the lie, leaves him.

MACDUFF

I believe drink gave thee the lie last night.

PORTER

That it did, Sir, it gripped me by the throat: but I threw him

up for his lie; and, I think, being too strong for him, though   35

he took my legs from under me, yet I made a shift to cock

him out.

MACDUFF

Is thy master stirring?

Macbeth enters

Our knocking has awaked him; here he comes.

Macduff exits

LENNOX

Good morrow, noble Sir!

MACBETH   Good morrow, both!   40

MACDUFF

Is the King stirring, worthy Thane?

MACBETH   Not yet.

MACDUFF

He did command me to call on him early:

I have almost missed the hour.

MACBETH   I'll bring you to him.

MACDUFF

I know this is a joyful trouble to you;

But yet 'tis one.   45

MACBETH

The labour we delight in pacifies pain.

This is the door.

MACDUFF

I must be so bold to call, for my time here is appointed.

Macduff exits

LENNOX

Goes the King hence today?

MACBETH

He does: he did expect to.   50

LENNOX

The night has been unruly: where we lay,

Our chimneys were blown down; and, as they say,

Lamentings heard i'th'air, strange screams of death,

And prophesying with terrible sounds,

Dreadful commotions, and confused events.   55

Newly hatch'd by woeful Nature, an Owl

Clamoured the livelong night: some say, the earth

Was feverish and did shake.

MACBETH   'Twas a rough night.

LENNOX

    My young remembrance has no memory

    To parallel it.   60

                      Macduff re-enters

MACDUFF

    O horror! horror! horror!

    Tongue nor heart cannot conceive, nor name thee!

MACBETH/LENNOX

    What's the matter?

MACDUFF

    Confusion now hath made his masterpiece!

    Most sacrilegious Murder has broke ope'   65

    The Lord's anointed Temple, and stole thence

    The life o'th'building!

MACBETH   What is't you say? The life?

LENNOX

    Mean you his Majesty?

MACDUFF

    Enter his chamber, and shatter your sight

    With a new Monster. Do not bid me speak —   70

    See, and then speak yourselves.

                  Macbeth and Lennox exit

                        Awake! Awake!

    Ring the alarm bell! Murder, and treason!

    Banquo, and Donalbain! Malcolm, awake!

    Shake off this downy sleep, death's imposter,

    And look on death itself! Up, up, and see   75

    The Last Judgment's form! Malcolm! Banquo!

    As from your graves rise up, and walk like ghosts,

    To aptly face this horror! Ring the bell!

                     Alarm bell rings

                 Lady Macbeth enters

LADY MACBETH

What's the business,

That such a hideous trumpet calls to alarm   80

The sleepers of the house? Speak, speak!

MACDUFF

O gentle lady,

'Tis not for you to hear what I must speak:

The repetition, in a woman's ear,

Would murder her to know it.

Banquo enters

O Banquo, Banquo,   85

Our royal master's murdered!

LADY MACBETH   Woe, alas!

What!? In our house?

BANQUO   Too cruel, anywhere.

Dear Duff, I pray thee contradict thyself,

And say it is not so.

Macbeth, Lennox and Ross enter

MACBETH

Had I but died an hour before this chance,   90

I had lived a blessed life; for, from this instant,

There's nothing serious in mortality;

All is but toys: renown, and grace, is dead;

The wine of life is drained, and the mere dregs

Are left for bitter boasting.   95

Malcolm and Donalbain enter

DONALBAIN

What is amiss?

MACBETH   You are, and do not know't:

The spring, the head, the fountain of your blood

Is stopped; the very source of it is stopped.

MACDUFF

Your royal father's murdered.

MALCOLM   NO! By whom?

LENNOX

His two chamber-men, it would seem had done't.   100

Their hands and faces were all badged with blood;

So were their daggers, which, unwiped, we found

Upon their pillows: they stared, gripped by madness;

No man's life was to be trusted with them.

MACBETH

Oh! Yet I do repent me of my fury,   105

That I did kill them.

MACDUFF   Why did you do so?

MACBETH

Who can be wise, amazed, temperate and furious,

Loyal and neutral, in such a moment? No man:

The swift voyage of my violent love

Outran that pauser, reason. Here lay Duncan,   110

His silver skin laced with his golden blood,

And his gashed stabs like sweet nature broken open

For ruin's wasteful entrance: there, the murderers,

Steeped in the colours of their trade, their daggers

Now cowards' tools, breeched with gore. Who'd refrain, 115

That had a heart to love, and in that heart

Courage to kill for love?

LADY MACBETH *(fainting)*

Heaven help me!

MACDUFF

Look to the Lady.

MALCOLM *(aside to Donalbain)*

Why do we hold our tongues, so they may claim   120

We put them up to it?

DONALBAIN *(aside to Malcolm)*

       What can be spoken

 Here, where our fate, hid in a witch's eye,

 May blink and seize us? Let's away,

 Our tears are not yet brewed.

MALCOLM *(aside to Donalbain)*

 Nor our strong sorrow   125

 Ready to be expressed.

BANQUO   Look to the Lady!

      Lady Macbeth is carried out

 And when our hearts and bodies are shielded,

 From painful exposure, let us meet,

 And question this most bloody piece of work,

 To know it further. Fears and Doubts shake us: 130

 In the great hand of God I stand, and thence

 Against the yet unknown motives I fight

 To right treason's malice.

MACDUFF   And so do I.

ALL   So all.

MACBETH

 Let's briefly put on manly readiness,

 And once armed, all meet in the hall.

ALL   Agreed.   135

   All but Malcolm and Donaldbain exit

MALCOLM

 What will you do? Let's not unite with them:

 To show an unfelt sorrow is a task

 Which the false man does easy. I'll to England.

DONALBAIN

 To Ireland, I; our separated fortune

 Shall keep us both the safer; where kin are,   140

 There's daggers in men's smiles; the near in blood,

The nearer bloody.

MALCOLM   This murderous shaft that's shot

Has not yet landed, and our safest way

Is to avoid the aim: therefore, to horse;

And let's be robust in our leave-taking,   145

Quick slip away. There's warrant in that theft

Which steals itself, when there's no mercy left.

Exit

ACT 2 ◆ SCENE 4

OUTSIDE THE CASTLE

Enter Ross and an Old Man

OLD MAN

Threescore and ten I can remember well,

And within all of that time I have seen

Hours dreadful, and things strange, but this sore night

Has beaten former knowings.

ROSS   Ha, good father,

Thou sees the heavens as troubled with man's act,   5

Threatens his bloody stage: by th'clock 'tis day,

And yet dark night strangles Sun's warm light.

Is it night's great power, or day's dire shame,

That Duncan's dark death does the earth entomb,

When light should kiss it awake?

OLD MAN   'Tis unnatural,   10

Even like the deed that's done. On Tuesday last,

A falcon, soaring in her place of pride,

Was stalked and killed by a mouse-hunting owl.

ROSS

And Duncan's horses a thing most strange and certain,

Beauteous and swift, the favoured of their race,   15

Turned wild in nature, broke their stalls, flung out,

39

Rebelling 'gainst obedience, as if they'd
Make war with mankind.

OLD MAN 'Tis said, they ate each other.

ROSS

They did so; to th'amazement of mine eyes,
That look'd upon't. 20

Enter Macduff

Here comes the good Macduff.

How goes the world, Sir, now?

MACDUFF Can you not see?!

ROSS

Is't known, who did this more than bloody deed?

MACDUFF

Those that Macbeth hath slain.

ROSS Oh wretched day!

What good could they pretend?

MACDUFF None. They were paid. 25

Malcolm and Donalbain, the King's two sons,
Are stolen away and fled; which puts upon them
Suspicion of the deed.

ROSS 'Gainst nature still:

Greedy Ambition, that will devour
Its own source of life! Then 'tis likely 30
The sovereignty will fall upon Macbeth.

MACDUFF

He is already named, and gone to Scone *{Skoon}*
To be invested for coronation.

ROSS

Where's Duncan's body?

MACDUFF Carried to Colmekill, *{Coomekill}*

The sacred storehouse of his predecessors, 35
And guardian of their bones.

ROSS   Will you to Scone? *{Skoon}*

MACDUFF

    No cousin; I'll to Fife.

ROSS   Well, I will go to Scone. *{Skoon}*

MACDUFF

    Well, may you see things well done there. Adieu!

    Lest our old rule prove easier than new.

ROSS

    Farewell, Father.   40

OLD MAN

    God's blessing go with you; and with those

    That would make good of bad, and friends of foes!

Exit

ACT 3 ◆ SCENE 1

FORRES. A ROOM IN THE KING'S PALACE

Enter Banquo dressed for riding

BANQUO *(to himself)*

You have it now, King, Cawdor *{Cordoor}*, Glamis *{Glarms}*, all,

As the Weïrd Women promis'd; and, I fear,

you play'dst most foully for't; yet it was said,

It should not crown your future heirs;

But that myself should be the root and father   5

Of many kings. If there come truth from them

As upon you, Macbeth, their speeches shine,

Why, by the verities on you made true,

May they not be my oracles as well

And raise my royal hopes? But, hush, no more.   10

Sennet (a trumpet call signaling a procession) is sounded

Enter Macbeth as King; Lady Macbeth, as Queen;

Lennox, Ross, Lords and Attendants

MACBETH

Here's our chief guest.

LADY MACBETH   If he had been forgotten,

It had been as a gap in our great feast,

A thing all too unbecoming.

MACBETH

Tonight we hold a stately supper, Sir,

And I'll request your presence.

BANQUO   Let your Highness   15

Command me, as it is to you my duties

Are with a most indissoluble tie

Forever knit.

MACBETH

Ride you this afternoon?

BANQUO   Ay, my good Lord.

MACBETH

We should have else desired your good advice   20

Which is as always both grave and prosperous

In today's council; but we'll wait till morrow.

Is't far you ride?

BANQUO

As far, my Lord, as will fill up the time

'Twixt this and supper. If my horse goes not faster,   25

I may become a borrower of the night,

For a dark hour, or two.

MACBETH   Fail not our feast.

BANQUO

My Lord, I will not.

MACBETH

We hear, our bloody cousins ran off, lodged

In England, and in Ireland; not confessing   30

Their cruel patricide, filling their hearers

With invented tales. But of that to-morrow,

When, besides, we will speak matters of State,

Concerning both. Hie you to horse: adieu,

Till you return at night. Goes Fleance with you?   35

BANQUO

Ay, my good Lord: our time does call upon's.

MACBETH

I wish your horses swift, and sure of foot;

And so I do deliver you to their backs.

Farewell.

Exit Banquo

Let every man be master of his time   40

Till seven tonight; to give our guests
The sweeter welcome. We keep to ourself
Alone till supper-time: God be with you.
Exit all except Macbeth and a Servant
Here, boy, a word with you.
Await those men our pleasure?   45
SERVANT
They do, my Lord, outside the palace gate.
MACBETH
Bring them before us.
Exit Servant. Macbeth speaks, referring to his crown
To be crowned is nothing, but to be safely so:
Our fears in Banquo stick deep,
And in his most royal nature reigns that   50
which would be feared. 'Tis much he dares,
And, to that dauntless temper of his mind,
He hath a wisdom that doth guide his valour
To act in safety. He is the one man
Whose being I do fear; and under him   55
My guiding spirit is rebuked; as,
Mark Antony's was by Caesar. He scoffed
When those Sisters spun the name of King on me,
And bade them speak to him; then, prophet-like,
They hail'd him father to a line of kings: 60
Upon my head they placed a childless crown,
And put a barren sceptre in my grip,
Thence to be wrench'd with an unlineal hand,
No son of mine succeeding. If 't be so,
For Banquo's issue have I fouled my mind;   65
For them the gracious Duncan have I murdered;
Placed bitter hate in my vessel of peace
Only for them; and my immortal soul

Given to Satan, Man's common Enemy,
To make them kings, the seeds of Banquo, kings!   70
Rather than so, come Fate into the fray,
And champion me even to my death! Who's there?

Re-enter Servant, with two Murderers

(to Servant)

Now, go to the door, and stay there till we call.

Exit Servant

(to Murderers)

Was it not yesterday we spoke together?

MURDERERS

It was, so please your Highness.

MACBETH   Well then,   75
Now have you considered what I have said?
Know, that it was he, in the times past,
Which made you so unfortunate,
Which you thought had been my innocent self?
This I made good to you in our last conference;   80
Proved beyond a doubt to you:
How he made you believe his false promises;
How betrayed; the tools he used to shape them,
And all things else, that might,
Make a half-wit, and a mind half-crazed,   85
Say, 'Thus did Banquo.'

MURDERER 1   You made it known to us.

MACBETH

I did so; and went further, which is now
The point of this second meeting. Does your
Patience so prevail over your nature
That you would let this go? Does your gospel   90
Preach you pray for this good man, and his child,
Whose heavy hand hath bent you early to your grave,

46

Made your kin beggars forever?

MURDERER 1   We are men, my Liege.

MACBETH

Ay, in the catalogue ye go for men;

As hounds, and greyhounds, mongrels, spaniels, curs,   95

Shags, water-rugs, and demi-wolves, are called

All by name of dogs: But the list of worth

Distinguishes the swift, the slow, the subtle,

The housekeeper, the hunter, every one

According to the gift which bounteous Nature   100

Hath thus bound him; whereby he does receive

Particular merits, from that docket

That writes them all alike; and so of men.

Now, if you have earned a place in that file,

Not i'th'worst rank of manhood, let's say,   105

Then I will plant that business in your bosoms

Whose execution takes your enemy off,

Clutches you to the heart and love of us,

Who wear our health uncertain in his life,

Which in his death were perfect.

MURDERER 2   I am one, my Liege,   110

Whom the vile blows and beatings of the world

Hath so enraged, that I am reckless what

I do to spite the world.

MURDERER 1   And I another,

So weary with disasters, mauled by fortune,

That I would set my life on any chance,   115

To mend it, or help end it.

MACBETH

Both of you know Banquo is your enemy.

MURDERER 2

True, my Lord.

47

MACBETH

So is he mine; and in such bloody discord,
That every minute of his being thrusts   120
Against all that lets me live: and though I could
With bare-faced power crush him into dust,
And with my crown assert it, yet I must not,
For certain friends that are both his and mine,
Whose loves I may not drop, will mourn his fall   125
Who I myself struck down: so here is why
I am making love to your assistance —
Masking the business from the public eye,
For sundry weighty reasons.

MURDERER 2   We shall, my Lord,
Perform what you command us.

MURDERER 1   Though our lives —   130

MACBETH

Your bravery shines through you.
Within this hour, at most,
I will advise you where to plant yourselves,
Acquaint you with the perfect place to spy
the perfect moment; for't must be done tonight,   135
And some ways from the palace: keep in mind,
That I must keep clear from blame: and with him
To leave no trace nor botches in the work,
Fleance his son, that keeps him company,
Whose "absence" is as important to us   140
As is his father's, must embrace the fate
Of that dark hour. Go now, resolve yourselves;
I'll come to you soon.

MURDERER 2   We are resolved, my lord.

MACBETH

I'll call on you shortly: go wait inside.

Exit Murderers

It is concluded: Banquo, thy soul's flight   145
If it find Heaven, must find it out tonight.

Exit

ACT 3 ◆ SCENE 2

THE SAME. ANOTHER ROOM

Enter Lady Macbeth and a Servant

LADY MACBETH

Is Banquo gone from court?

SERVANT

Ay, Madam, but returns again tonight.

LADY MACBETH

Say to the King, I await him when pleases

For a few words.

SERVANT   Madam, I will.

Exit Servant

LADY MACBETH

Nothing's gained, all's spent,   5

When desire's attained without content:

'Tis safer to be him which we destroy,

Than by destruction dwell in doubtful joy.

Enter Macbeth

How now, my Lord? Why keep you to yourself?

Your companions are inventing some sorry stories   10

Using those thoughts which should have died

With the dead to doubt us. Things without remedy

Should be without regard: what's done is done.

MACBETH

We have slashed the snake, not killed it:

She'll heal, and be herself; whilst our poor misdeeds   15

Remain in danger of her former bite.

49

Better the Universe fracture,
So both Heaven and Earth suffer,
Rather than eat our meals in fear, and sleep
In the affliction of these terrible dreams, 20
That shake us nightly: Better t'be with the dead,
Whom we, to gain our peace, have sent to peace,
Than to torture our minds as they are pulled apart
Into sleepless frenzy. Duncan in his grave;
After life's fitful fever, sleeps well; 25
Treason has done his worst: not steel, nor poison,
Not his countrymen's hate, nor foreign armies,
Nothing can touch him further!

LADY MACBETH   Come on: Calm down my Lord,
Smooth over your rough looks; Be bright and jovial
Among your guests to-night. 30

MACBETH
So shall I, Love; and so, I pray, will you.
Let your attention apply to Banquo:
Treat him with esteem, of both eye and tongue:
In these unsafe times, we must now
Wash our honours in these flattering streams, 35
And make our faces calm masks to our hearts,
Disguising what they are.

LADY MACBETH   You must stop this.

MACBETH
O, full of scorpions is my mind, dear wife:
Thou know'st that Banquo, and his Fleance, lives.

LADY MACBETH
Yes, but Nature has not made them immortal. 40

MACBETH
There's comfort yet; they are assailable:
Then be joyful. Before the bat has flown

His cloistered flight; Before the dung beetle
With his drowsy hums, has rung Night's yawning bell
At black Hecate's summons, there shall be done   45
A deed of dreadful note.

LADY MACBETH   What's to be done?

MACBETH

Be innocent of the knowledge, dearest Chuck,
Till thou applaud the deed. Come, sewn-tight Night,
Inveil the tender eye of pitiful Day
And, with thy bloody and invisible hand   50
Cancel, and tear to pieces that moral bond
Which keeps me pale! Night thickens; and the crow
Makes wing to his rooky wood;
Good things of Day begin to droop and drowse,
Whiles Night's black agents their preys do rouse.   55
Thou marvell'st at my words: but hold thee still;
Things bad begun are made stronger by ill.
So, please I pray, stand with me today.

Exit

ACT 3 ◆ SCENE 3

THE SAME. A PARK, WITH A ROAD LEADING TO THE PALACE

Enter three Murderers

MURDERER 1

But who did bid thee join with us?

MURDERER 3 *(Macbeth)*   Macbeth.

MURDERER 2

We need not mistrust him since he delivers
Our orders to us, and all we must do
Just as we were told.

MURDERER 1   Then stand with us.
The west yet glimmers with some streaks of day;   5

Now spurring on the belated traveller
To speed to the castle; and near approaches
The subject of our watch.

MURDERER 3 *(Macbeth)*   Hark! I hear horses.

BANQUO *(offstage)*

Give us a light there!

MURDERER 2   Then 'tis he: the rest

On the list of invited guests   10

Are already there.

MURDERER 1   His horses go about.

MURDERER 3 *(Macbeth)*

Almost a mile with the grooms, usually.
But all men do, from hence to palace gate
Walk along here.

Enter Banquo, and Fleance, with a torch

MURDERER 2

A light, a light!

MURDERER 3 *(Macbeth)*   'Tis he.   15

MURDERER 1

Stand to't.

BANQUO   It will be rain tonight.

MURDERER 1   Let it come down.

BANQUO

O, treachery!

The First Murderer strikes out the light,
while the others assault Banquo

Fly, good Fleance, fly, fly, fly!
Thou must revenge —

Fleance escapes
O slave!
Banquo dies

MURDERER 3 *(Macbeth)*

Who did strike out the light?

MURDERER 1   Was't not the plan?   20

MURDERER 3 *(Macbeth)*

There's but one down: the son is fled.

MURDERER 2   We have lost

Best half of our affair.

MURDERER 1   Well, let's away,

And say how much is done.

Exit

ACT 3 ◆ SCENE 4

A STATEROOM IN THE PALACE

A banquet prepared. Enter Macbeth, Lady Macbeth, Ross, Lennox,
Lords, and Attendants

MACBETH

You know your earned places, sit down. To one and all,

A hearty welcome.

LORDS   Thanks to your Majesty.

MACBETH

Ourself will mingle with society,

And play the humble host.

Our hostess keeps her throne; but, now,   5

We will require her give you welcome.

LADY MACBETH

Proclaim it for me, Sir, to all our friends;

For my heart speaks, they are welcome.

Enter Murderer 1, to the door

MACBETH

See, they encounter thee with their hearts' thanks.

Both sides are even: here I'll sit i'th'midst.   10

53

Enjoy yourselves; Soon, we'll drink a toast
Around the table.

Goes to door, speaks to Murderer 1. Only HE sees or hears him.

There's blood upon thy face.

MURDERER 1

'Tis Banquo's then.

MACBETH   'Tis better outside you, than inside him.

Is he dispatch'd?   15

MURDERER 1

My Lord, his throat is cut; that I did for him.

MACBETH

Thou art the best o'th'cut-throats;

Yet bester who did the like for Fleance:

If thou didst it, thou art the nonpareil. *{nonparay}*

MURDERER 1

Most royal Sir, Fleance is 'scaped.   20

MACBETH

Then comes my fit again: I had else been perfect;

Whole as the marble, firm-set as the rock,

As free and untethered as the flowing air:

But now, I am cabined, cribbed, confined, bound

By brazen doubts and fears. But Banquo's safe?   25

MURDERER 1

Ay, my good Lord, safe in a ditch he bides,

With twenty trenched gashes on his head;

Each one a death to nature.

MACBETH   Thanks for that.

There the grown serpent lies; that worm that's fled

Hath nature that in time will venom breed,   30

Hath no teeth for now. Get thee gone, tomorrow

We'll speak together again.

Exit Murderer 1

LADY MACBETH   My royal Lord,
    You did not give the toast: the feast is frigid
    That is not plainly pledged while in the making.
    Without this welcome, twere best to feed at home: 35
    From thence, the sauce to meat is ceremony,
    Meetings are bare without it.
          The Ghost of Banquo enters, and sits in Macbeth's place
MACBETH   Sweet remembrancer!
    Now, good digestion attend appetite,
    And health on both!
LENNOX   May it please your Highness sit?
MACBETH
    Under one roof, we would have all our honour   40
    Were the graced person of our Banquo present,
    Who I hope only to scold for unkindness,
    Not mourn for his misfortune!
ROSS   His absence, Sir,
    Proves his broken promise. Would your Highness
    Please grace us with your royal company?   45
MACBETH
    The table's full.
LENNOX   Here is a place reserved, Sir.
MACBETH   Where?
LENNOX
    Here, my good Lord. What is't that moves your Highness?
          Now Macbeth sees fully the Ghost of Banquo
MACBETH
    Which of you have done this?
LORDS   What, my good Lord?
MACBETH
    Thou cannot say, I did it: *(to Banquo's Ghost)* never shake
    Thy gory locks at me.   50

ROSS

Gentlemen, rise; His Highness is not well.

LADY MACBETH

Sit, worthy friends. My Lord is often thus,

And hath been from his youth: pray you, keep seat,

The fit is momentary; soon enough

He will again be well. Take no note of him.   55

You shall offend him, and extend his outburst.

Eat, and regard him not. *(To Macbeth)* Are you a man?

MACBETH

Ay, and a bold one, that dare look on that

Which might appall the Devil.

LADY MACBETH   Oh, such nonsense!

This is the very painting of your fear: 60

This is the air-drawn dagger that you said,

Led you to Duncan. Oh! These fits and starts,

Impostors to true fear, would well become

A woman's story at a winter's fire,

Authorized by her grandmum. Shame itself!   65

Why do you make such faces? When all's done,

You look but on a chair.

MACBETH   Prithee, see there!

Behold! Look! How say you?

(to the Ghost)

Why, what care I? If thou can nod, speak too.

If bone-filled vaults and graves must send   70

Those we bury back, the bellies of preying birds

Become their monuments.

Ghost of Banquo disappears

LADY MACBETH

What!? Quite unmanned in folly.

MACBETH

As I stand here, I saw him.

LADY MACBETH   Fie, for shame!

MACBETH

Blood hath been shed from now to olden times,   75

Though humane laws made a civilized state;

We still have savage murders being dispatched

Too terrible for the ear: the time has been,

That, when the brains were out, the man would die,

And there's an end; but now, they rise again,   80

With twenty lethal lashes on their heads,

And push us from our chairs. This is more strange

Than such a murder is.

LADY MACBETH   My worthy Lord,

Your noble friends await you.

MACBETH   I do forget.

Do not muse at me, my most worthy friends,   85

I have a strange infirmity, which is nothing

To those that know me. Come, love and health to all,

Then, I'll sit down. Give me some wine, fill full.

Re-enter Banquo's Ghost

I drink to the general joy o'th whole table,

And to our dear friend Banquo, whom we miss —   90

Would he were here. To all, and him we thirst,

And all to all.

LORDS   Our duties, and the pledge.

MACBETH *(to Banquo's Ghost)*

Be gone! And quit my sight! Let the earth hide thee.

Thy bones are marrowless, thy blood is cold;

Thou hast no speculation in those eyes   95

With which thou dost glare.

LADY MACBETH   Think of this, good Peers,

But as a thing of custom: 'tis no other;

Only it spoils the pleasure of the time.

MACBETH

What man dare, I dare.

Approach thou like the rugged Russian bear,   100

The armed rhinoceros, or fierce Hyrcan tiger;

Take any shape but that, and my firm nerves

Shall never tremble: or, be alive again,

And dare me to the desert with thy sword;

If trembling is my habit then, pronounce me   105

A girl's baby-doll. Hence, horrible shadow!

Unreal mockery, Go!

Ghost of Banquo disappears

Why so being gone

I am a man again. *(To the Lords)* Pray you, sit still.

LADY MACBETH

You have ruined the mirth, broke the good meeting

With most amazing disorder.

MACBETH   Can such things be,   110

And overcome us like a summer's cloud,

Without our special wonder? You make me

Doubt my own true character and nature,

When now I think you can behold such sights,

And keep the natural ruby of your cheeks,   115

When mine is blanched with fear.

ROSS   What sights, my Lord?

LADY MACBETH

I pray you, speak not; he grows worse and worse;

Questions enrage him. At once, good night.

Stand not upon the order of your going,

But go at once.

LENNOX   Good night, and better health   120
   Attend his Majesty!
LADY MACBETH   A kind good night to all!
        Exit Lords and Attendants
MACBETH
   It will have blood, they say: blood will have blood:
   Stones have been known to move, and trees to speak;
   Prophesies by those who know connections, have
   By mag-pies, and crows, and rooks revealed   125
   The secret'st murderer. What is the night?
LADY MACBETH
   Almost at odds with morning, which is which.
MACBETH
   Why dost thou think Macduff denies his presence
   At our great bidding?
LADY MACBETH   Did you send to him, Sir?
MACBETH
   I heard it spoken; but I will send note.   130
   There's no servant to spare but in his house
   I keep a watchman paid. I will to-morrow
   Go early to meet with the Weïrd Sisters.
   More shall they speak: for now I am bent to know
   In the worst way, the worst; for mine own good,   135
   Nothing shall halt my way. I am in blood
   Stepped in so far, that, should I wade no further,
   Returning were as bloody as crossing over.
   Strange things I have in head, that will to hand,
   Which must be acted, ere they may be scanned.   140
LADY MACBETH
   You lack the season of all natures, sleep.
MACBETH
   Come, we'll to sleep. My strange and self-abuse

Is the novice's fear that lacks hard use.

We are yet but young in deed.

Exit

ACT 3 ◆ SCENE 5

THE HEATH

Thunder. Enter Witch 1, meeting Hecate

WITCH 1

Why, how now, Hecate? You look angerly.

As Hecate speaks, Witches 2 & 3 sneak off to chant/sing a ditty that
will make Hecate leave. Witch 1 can spur them on silently.

HECATE

Have I not reason, hag-rags that you are,

Saucy, and overbold? How did you dare

To trade and traffic with Macbeth,

In riddles, and affairs of death;   5

And I, the mistress of your charms,

The closed contriver of all harms,

Was never called to bear my part

Or show the glory of our art?

And, which is worse, all you have done   10

Hath been but for a wayward son,

But make amends now: get you gone,

At the mouth of Hell's Acheron

Meet by that river; thither he

Will come to know his destiny.   15

Your vessels, and your spells, provide,

Your charms, and everything beside.

I am flying; this night I'll spend

Weaving a dismal and a fatal end.

He shall spurn fate, scorn death, and bear   20

His hopes 'bove wisdom, grace, and fear;

And as you know, security
Is mortals' greatest enemy.
Chanted Song offstage for Witches 2 & 3 to get Hecate to leave

WITCHES 2 & 3

Dark Queen come 'fore the Sun doth rise,
We'll taste your lips and kiss your sighs. 25
Dark Queen come when the moon is new
Let red-toothed creatures drink your dew.

HECATE

Hark! I am called: my little spirit, see,
Sits in a foggy cloud, and waits for me.
Exit Hecate as Witches 2 & 3 enter quietly,
so Hecate cannot see

WITCH 1

Come, let's make haste: she'll soon be back again. 30
The three Witches Exit
INTERMISSION

ACT 3 ◆ SCENE 6

SOMEWHERE IN SCOTLAND
Enter Lennox and another Lord

LENNOX

My former speeches have but touched your thoughts,
Which I can interpret farther. I say
Things have been strangely borne. The gracious Duncan
Was pitied by Macbeth after he was dead.
And the right-valiant Banquo walked after dark 5
Whom, you may say, if't please you, Fleance killed,
For Fleance fled. Men must not walk too late.
Who cannot lack the thought, how monstrous
It was for Malcolm, and for Donalbain,
To kill their gracious father? Damned fact! 10

How it did grieve Macbeth! Did he not just
In pious rage, tear the two delinquent grooms,
That were the slaves of drink, enthralled with sleep?
Was not that nobly done? Ay, and wisely too:
For 'twould have angered any heart alive 15
To hear the men deny't. So that, I say,
He has done all things well: and I do think,
That, had he Duncan's sons under his key
And, if please Heaven, he shall not, they should find
What it were to kill a father; so should Fleance. 20
Enough! For from broad words, and 'cause he failed
His presence at the tyrant's feast, I hear,
Macduff lives in disgrace. Sir, can you tell
Where he hides himself?

LORD

Duncan's son, Malcolm, 25
From whom Macbeth has stole his true birth right,
Lives in the English court; and is received
By the pious King Edward with such grace,
That the malevolence of fortune cannot
Take away his high respect. And there Macduff 30
Is gone to beg the holy King,
To wake Northumberland, and warlike Siward; {See-word}
And, by this allegiance, with God above
To ratify the work, we may again
Give to our tables meat, sleep to our nights, 35
Free our feasts and banquets from bloody knives,
Do faithful homage, and receive free honours,
All which we pine for now. And this report
Has so exasperated Macbeth, that he
Prepares for some attempt at war. 40

LENNOX

Sent he to Macduff?

LORD

He did: and with an absolute 'Sir, not I,'

The scowling messenger turns his back,

And hums, as if to say, 'You'll rue the time

You gave me this answer.'

LENNOX   And that well might   45

Advise him to keep what distance from Scotland

His wisdom provides. May a swift Angel

Fly to the court of England, and unfold

The blessed message that he quickly return,

To this our suffering country   50

And free us from Macbeth's accursed hand!

LORD

I would send my prayers with him.

Exit

ACT 4 ◆ SCENE 1

OUTSIDE THE PALACE GROUNDS, PERHAPS IN A CAVE

*From the shadows we hear the Three Witches singing like something
out of Tim Burton's "Corpse Bride"*

ALL

Who prays to whom on purple heath

WITCH 1

When moon is full, we see Macbeth.

WITCH 2

He carries secrets in his veins

WITCH 3 *(like a punk-rock song)*

Let's pierce his skin and stroke his pains.

In the middle, a boiling cauldron
Thunder. Enter the three Witches

WITCH 1

Thrice the mottled cat hath mewed.   5

WITCH 2

Twice and once the hedgehog whined.

Witch 3's familiar, a "Harpier," makes the sound of a magpie cawing

WITCH 3

My magpie cries: 'Tis time, 'tis time.

WITCH 1

Round about the cauldron go;

In the poison'd entrails throw.

Toad, that under cold stone   10

Days and nights has thirty-one

Oozing venom, sleeping got,

Boil thou first i'th'charmèd pot.

ALL

Double, double toil and trouble:

Fire, burn; and, cauldron, bubble.   15

WITCH 2

Fillet of a forest snake,

In the cauldron boil and bake;

Eye of newt, and toe of frog,

Wool of bat, and tongue of dog,

Adder's fork, and blind-worm's sting,   20

Lizard's leg, and owlet's wing,

For a charm of powerful trouble,

Like a hell-broth boil and bubble.

ALL

Double, double toil and trouble:

Fire, burn; and, cauldron, bubble.   25

WITCH 3

Scale of dragon, tooth of wolf;

Witches' mummy; craw and gulf

Of the glutted salt-sea shark;

Root of hemlock, dug i'th'dark;

Liver of blaspheming Jew;   30

Gall of goat, and slips of yew,

Sliver'd in the moon's eclipse;

Nose of Turk, and Tartar's lips;

Finger of birth-strangled Moor

Ditch-deliver'd by a whore   35

Make the gruel thick with gore,

Add thereto a tiger's organ

For th'ingredients of our cauldron.

ALL

Double, double toil and trouble:

Fire, burn; and, cauldron, bubble.   40

WITCH 2

Cool it with a baboon's blood:

Then the charm is firm and good.

Enter Hecate

HECATE

O, well done! I commend your pains,

And every one shall share i'th'gains.

And now about the cauldron sing,   45

Like elves and fairies in a ring,

Enchanting all that you put in.

Music, like from a 60s girl group, plays and the Witches sing

Modeled after "Foolish Little Girl" and "Sha-la-la" by the Shirelles

WITCH 1 *(spoken intro)*

Sisters, gather 'round a spell.

Hecate wants us now to tell,

A story of witchy glory —   50

Spun by fate and oh so gory.

WITCH 2 & 3

Sha-la-la-la-la-la-la, sha-la-la-la-la-la-la-la

Sha-la-la-la-la, sha-la-la-la-la

Woah, woah, woah, woah.

WITCH 1

Macbeth comes for counsel late tonight,   55

We'll give him a Crown fitted tight.

WITCH 1, 2 & 3

Knock him down with his own ambitions,

Squeeze Blood from his nocturnal emissions.

He'll pour into our potion —

Make it thick with emotion.   60

WITCH 2

Oh, tug and pull till he screams —

Men have such short-haired seams.

WITCH 3

Oh cream and steam till he wails,

Blowing up our pussy tails.

WITCH 2 & 3

Sha-la-la-la-la-la, sha-la-la-la-la-la-la-la   65

Sha-la-la-la-la, sha-la-la-la-la

Woah, woah, woah, woah.

WITCH 1, 2 & 3

That's how we'll roll that guy —

The one with wanting eyes …

WITCH 2

Weave a spell of brains and sighs …   70

WITCH 3

Make stew of his bones and thighs.

WITCH 1, 2 & 3

Sha-la-la-la-la-la-la, sha-la-la-la-la-la-la-la

Sha-la-la-la-la, sha-la-la-la-la

(spoken) Men sin when Weird Sisters spin.

Hecate stops the song with her words

HECATE

HARK! A black spirit hovers near.   75

Show him all and he'll soon fall.

Exit Hecate

WITCH 2

By the pricking of my thumbs,

WITCH 3

Something wicked this way comes.

WITCH 1

Open locks, whoever knocks.

The Witches laugh & meow. Enter Macbeth

MACBETH

How now, you secret, black, and midnight hags!   80

What is't you do?

ALL   A deed without a name.

MACBETH

   I entreat you, to use all you profess,

   Howe'er you come to know it, answer me;

   Though you untie the winds, and let them fight

   Against the Churches, though the foamy waves   85

   Confound and swallow up all ships that sail,

   Though new corn you crush, and trees blow down,

   Then castles topple on their keepers' heads,

   Though palaces and pyramids do bend

   Their heads to their foundations; though the treasure   90

   Of Nature's life sources tumble so completely

   As to sicken destruction, answer me

   All what I ask you.

      The Witches speak as if performing an unsettling seduction

WITCH 1   Speak.

WITCH 2   Demand.

WITCH 3   We'll answer.

WITCH 1

   Say, if thou'dst rather hear it from our mouths…

WITCH 1, 2 & 3

   Or from our masters?

MACBETH   Call 'em; let me see 'em.   95

WITCH 1

   Pour in sow's blood, that hath eaten

   Her nine piglets; Torn flesh, taken

   From the murderer's gallows, throw

   Into the flame.

ALL   Come, high, or low;

   Thyself and duty deftly show.   100

     Thunder. First Apparition, an armed head, ascends from below

MACBETH

Tell me, thou unknown power —

WITCH 1   He knows thy thought:

Hear his speech, but say thou nought.

APPARITION 1

Macbeth, Macbeth, Macbeth: Beware Macduff,

Beware the Thane of Fife. Dismiss me. Enough.

Apparition 1 descends

MACBETH

Whate'er thou art, for thy good caution, thanks;   105

Thou hast guessed my fear aright. But one word more —

WITCH 1

He will not be commanded.

WITCH 2   Here's another,

WITCH 2

More potent than the first.

Thunder. Second Apparition, a bloody child, ascends

APPARITION 2

Macbeth. Macbeth. Macbeth.

MACBETH

Had I three ears, I'd hear thee.   110

APPARITION 2

Be bloody, bold, and resolute: laugh to scorn

The power of man, for none of woman born

Shall harm Macbeth.

Apparition 2 descends

MACBETH

Then live, Macduff: what need I fear of thee?

But yet I'll make assurance double sure,   115

And make a bond with Fate: he shalt not live,

So I may tell pale-hearted fear it lies,

And sleep in spite of thunder.

Thunder

Apparition 3, a crowned child, with a tree branch in his hand, ascends

What is this

That rises like the offspring of a king;

And wears upon his baby brow the round   120

Gold crown of sovereignty?

ALL WITCHES   Listen, but speak not to't.

APPARITION 3

Be lion-mettled, proud, and take no care

Who chafes, who frets, or where conspirers are:

Macbeth shall not defeated be until

Great Birnam wood to high Dunsinane Hill   125

Shall rise against him.

Apparition 3 descends

MACBETH   That will never be.

Who can enlist the forest, bid the tree

Unfix his earth-bound root? Sweet omens, good.

Rebellious dead, rise never till the wood

Of Birnam rise, and our high-placed Macbeth   130

Shall live life's natural course, lose his breath

To time, and mortal custom. Yet my heart

Throbs to know one thing: tell me, if your art

Can tell so much, shall Banquo's offspring ever

Reign in this kingdom?

ALL   Seek to know no more.   135

MACBETH

I will be satisfied. Deny me this,

and an eternal curse fall on you! Let me know.

Why sinks that cauldron —

The sound of Oboes

— and what noise is this?

WITCH 1

Here's

WITCH 2

Your   140

WITCH 3

Show!

ALL

Show his eyes, and grieve his heart;

Come like shadows, so depart.

> *A show of eight Kings, the last with a mirror-glass in his hand;*
> *Banquo follows*

MACBETH

Thou art too like the spirit of Banquo. Down!

Thy crown does sear mine eyeballs.

(to the second in line)   And thy hair,   145

Another gold-bound brow, so like the first.

A third is like the former. Filthy hags!

Why do you show me this? A fourth! Burn, eyes!

What, will the line stretch out to th'crack of doom?

Another yet! A seventh! I'll see no more: 150

And yet the eighth appears, who holds a glass

Which shows me many more; and some I see

Carry Scotland's orbs and the scepters of Wales.

Horrible sight! Now I see, 'tis true;

For the blood-blackened Banquo smiles upon me   155

And points at them as his.

> *Exit Kings and Banquo*
> What? Is this so?

WITCH 1

Ay, Sir, all this is so. But why

Stands Macbeth thus amazedly?

Come, sisters, cheer we up his sprites,

And show the best of our delights.   160
WITCH 2

   I'll charm the air to give a sound,

   While you perform your frantic round;
WITCH 3

   That this "great King" may kindly say,

   Our duties gave him welcome pay.

Music. The Witches dance, and vanish

MACBETH

   Where are they? Gone? Let this malignant hour   165

   Stand so accursed in the calendar!

   You without, come in!

Enter Lennox

LENNOX   What's your Grace's will?
MACBETH

   Saw you the weïrd sisters?
LENNOX   No, my Lord.
MACBETH

   Came they not by you?
LENNOX   No, indeed, my Lord.
MACBETH

   Infected be the air whereon they ride;   170

   And damned all those that trust them! I did hear

   The galloping of horse. Who was't came by?
LENNOX

   'Tis two or three, my Lord, that bring you word,

   Macduff is fled to England.
MACBETH   Fled to England?
LENNOX

   Ay, my good Lord.   175
MACBETH *(aside)*

   Time, thou anticipates my dread exploits.

The racing purpose never is undertook
Unless the deed follows close. From this moment,
The very firstlings in my heart shall be
The firstlings of my hand. Even now I must   180
Crown my thoughts with acts, as soon as thought it's done.
The castle of Macduff I will surprise,
Seize upon Fife, give th'edge o'th'sword to
His wife, his babes, and all unfortunate souls
That trace his family line. No boasting like a fool;   185
This deed I'll do before this purpose cool.
Visions be gone!

(to Lennox)

Where are these gentlemen?
Come, bring me where they are.

Exit Macbeth and Lennox

ACT 4 ◆ SCENE 2

FIFE. A ROOM IN MACDUFF'S CASTLE

Enter Lady Macduff, her Son, and Ross

LADY MACDUFF

What had he done, to make him fly the land?

ROSS

You must have patience, Madam.

LADY MACDUFF   He had none;

His flight was madness. Though our actions do not,
Our fears do make us traitors.

ROSS   You know not

Whether it was Macduff's wisdom, or his fear.   5

LADY MACDUFF

Wisdom? To leave his wife, to leave his babes,
His mansion, and his titles, in a place
From whence himself does fly? He loves us not;

He lacks Nature's warmth; even the poor wren,
The most diminutive of birds, will fight   10
Against the owl, for young ones in her nest.
All is the fear, and nothing is the love;
As little is his wisdom, where his flight
So runs against all reason.
ROSS   My dearest coz,
I pray you, calm yourself: keep faith. Your husband,   15
He is noble, wise, judicious, and best knows
The ways of the world. I dare not speak much further;
But cruel are the times, when we are traitors
And do not know ourselves; believing rumours
Based on what we fear, yet know not what we fear,   20
But float upon a wild and violent sea
Lurching side to side. I take my leave, Cuz.
Shall not be long but I'll be here again.
Things at the worst will cease, or else climb upward
To what they were before. *(To the Son)* My young Macduff,   25
Blessing upon you.
LADY MACDUFF
Fathered he is, and yet he's fatherless.
ROSS
I am so much a fool, should I stay longer,
Tears would be my disgrace, and your discomfort:
I take my leave at once.

Exit Ross

LADY MACDUFF   Young man, your father's dead: 30
And what will you do now? How will you live?
SON
As birds do, mother.
LADY MACDUFF   What, with worms and flies?

SON

    With what I get, I mean; and so do they.

LADY MACDUFF

    Poor bird! Thou have never feared the net, nor lime,

    The set trap, nor the snare.

SON   Why should I, mother?   35

    Poor birds are never hunted.

    My father is not dead, whatever you say.

LADY MACDUFF

    Yes, he is dead: what wilt thou do for a father?

SON

    Nay, what will you do for a husband?

LADY MACDUFF

    Why, I can buy me twenty at any market.   40

SON

    Then you'll buy 'em to sell again.

LADY MACDUFF

    Thou speaks with all thy wit;

    And yet, in faith, with wit enough for thee.

SON

    Was my father a traitor, mother?

LADY MACDUFF

    Ay, that he was.   45

SON

    What is a traitor?

LADY MACDUFF

    Why, one that swears and lies.

SON

    And be all traitors that do so?

LADY MACDUFF

    Every one that does so is a traitor, and must be hanged.

SON

  And must they all be hanged that swear and lie?   50

LADY MACDUFF

  Every one.

SON

  Who must hang them?

LADY MACDUFF

  Why, the honest men.

SON

  Then the liars and swearers are fools; for there are enough

  liars and swearers to beat the honest men, and hang them first. 55

LADY MACDUFF

  Now God help thee, poor monkey! But what wilt thou do for a

      father?

SON

  If he were dead, you'd weep for him: if you would not, it were

  a good sign that I should quickly have a new father.

LADY MACDUFF

  Poor prattler, how thou talks!

Enter a Messenger

MESSENGER

  Bless you, fair dame! I am not to you known,   60

  Though of your state of honour I well know.

  I fear some danger does approach you nearly.

  If you will take a simple man's advice,

  Be not found here; flee with your little ones.

  To fright you thus, methinks, I am too savage;   65

  To not warn you thus were worse cruelty,

  When tis so near upon you. Heaven preserve you!

  I dare remain no longer.

Exit Messenger

LADY MACDUFF

Where then should I fly?
I have done no harm. But I remember now   70
I am in this earthly world, where, to do harm
Is often laudable; to do good, sometime
Accounted dangerous folly: why then, alas!
Do I put up that womanly defence,
To say I have done no harm?

Enter Murderers

What are these men?   75

MURDERER 1

Where is your husband?

LADY MACDUFF

I hope, in no place so unsanctified,
Where such as thou may find him.

MURDERER 1   He's a traitor.

SON

Thou liest, thou shag-haired villain!

MURDERER 1   What, you egg!

Stabbing him

Young fry of treachery!

SON   He has killed me, mother: 80

Run away, I pray you!

Son Dies

Exit Lady Macduff, crying 'Murder!' and pursued by the Murderers

ACT 4 ◆ SCENE 3

ENGLAND. A ROOM IN THE ENGLISH KING'S PALACE

Enter Malcolm and Macduff

MALCOLM

Let us seek out some barren shade, and there
Weep our sad bosoms empty.

MACDUFF   Prince Malcolm, let's
  Hold fast our deadly swords, and like good men
  Protect our fallen homeland. Each new morn,
  New widows howl, new orphans cry; new sorrows   5
  Strike heaven on the face, so it resounds
  As if it felt with Scotland, and yelled out
  Like the cry of our deep pain.
MALCOLM   What I believe, I'll wail;
  What know, believe; and what I can redress,
  As I shall find the time to is right, I will.   10
  This tyrant, whose name alone blisters tongues,
  You may see something of him in me, and seek
  Wisely to offer me up, a weak lamb
  T'appease that angry and dishonest god.
MACDUFF
  I am not treacherous.
MALCOLM   But Macbeth is.   15
  A good and virtuous nature may recoil
  From a royal command. But I shall crave your pardon;
  My thoughts cannot transform you Lord Macduff.
  Angels shine though brightest Lucifer fell:
  Though all things foul would wear the face of grace,   20
  Yet Grace must still look fair.
MACDUFF   I have lost my hopes.
MALCOLM
  Perhaps that same place where I did find my doubts.
  Why in that danger left you wife and child —
  Those precious kindred, those strong knots of love —
  Without leave-taking? I pray you,   25
  Let not my suspicions show you dishonor,
  But my own safeguards. You may be a good man
  Whatever I might think.

MACDUFF   Bleed, bleed, poor country.
  Great Tyranny, set down firmly your base,
  For goodness dare not check thee. Wear thou well thy wrongs; 30
  Thy title is confirmed. Fare thee well, Prince:
  I would not be the villain that thou think'st
  For all of Scotland in the tyrant's grasp,
  And the rich East to boot.

MALCOLM
  Be not offended: 35
  Our country sinks beneath his brutal yoke;
  It weeps, it bleeds; and each new day a gash
  Is added to her wounds: I think, also,
  There would be hands uplifted for our fight;
  Here gracious Edward of England offers me 40
  Some goodly thousand men. But for all this,
  When I shall tread upon the tyrant's head,
  Or wear it on my sword, yet my poor country
  Shall have more vices than it had before,
  Suffering in more sundry ways than ever, 45
  By him that shall succeed.

MACDUFF   Who should he be?

MALCOLM
  It is myself I mean; in whom I know
  All the particulars of vice so implanted
  That, when they shall be cut open, black Macbeth
  Will seem as pure as snow; and the poor State 50
  Esteem him as a lamb, being compared
  With my limitless harms.

MACDUFF   Not in the legions
  Of horrid Hell can come a devil more damned
  In evils, to top Macbeth.

MALCOLM

   I grant him smacking of every sin   55

   That has a name; but there's no bottom, none,

   In my dire debauchery. Your wives, your daughters,

   Your matrons, and your maids, could not fill up

   The cistern of my lust; and my desire

   All chaste and pure impediments would o'ertake,   60

   That did oppose my will: better Macbeth,

   Than such as I to reign.

MACDUFF   Excessive indulgence

   In nature is a tyranny; it hath wrought

   Th'untimely destruction of the happy throne,

   And fall of many kings. But do not fear   65

   To take upon you what is yours. You may

   Pursue your pleasures in such abundance

   And yet seem pure. The time you may so hoodwink.

   There's no vulture in you hungry enough

   To devour as many dames as willing   70

   To surrender their own virtue to greatness

   If they feel so inclined.

MALCOLM   Along with lust,

   There grows an ill-composed temperament such

   An endless avarice, that, were I King,

   I should cut down the nobles for their lands,   75

   And my more-taking would be as a sauce

   To make me hunger more; that I should forge

   Quarrels unjust against the good and loyal,

   Destroying them for wealth.

MACDUFF   This avarice

   Digs deeper, grows with more ruinous root   80

   Than summer-lasting lust; and it hath been

   The sword which slayed our kings. Yet do not fear;

Scotland has the sources to fill up your will
Fully on her own. All can be endured
When weighed with your graces.   85

MALCOLM

But I have none. The king-becoming graces,
Like Justice, Honesty, Patience, Courage,
I have no relish of them, but abound
In the division of each and ev'ry crime,
Enacting them many ways. Nay, had I power, I should   90
Pour the sweet milk of Heaven into Hell,
Uproot our universal peace, crushing
All unity on earth.

MACDUFF   O Scotland! Scotland!

MALCOLM

If such a one be fit to govern, speak:
I am as I have spoken.

MACDUFF   Fit to govern?   95
Not fit to live. O nation miserable!
An unentitled tyrant bloody-sceptred,
When shalt Scotland see wholesome days again,
Since the true inheritor of your throne
By his own admission stands accursed,   100
And does defame his family? Your royal father
Was a most sainted King: the Queen that bore thee,
Oft'ner knelt to God than stood on her feet,
Died to be reborn every day she lived. Fare you well.
These evils you recount into mine ears   105
Have banished me from Scotland. O my breast,
Thy hope ends here.

MALCOLM   Macduff, your noble passion,
Child of integrity, has from my soul
Wiped the blackened doubts, reconciled my thoughts

To thy good truth and honour.
                              Here renounce   110
The taints and blames I laid upon myself,
As strangers to my nature. I am yet
To know a woman; Never broke my word,
Scarcely have coveted what was my own,
At no time broke my faith, would not betray   115
The Devil to his fellow; and delight
In truth as much as life: my first false speaking
Was now about myself. What I am truly,
Is thine, and my poor country's, to command.
Whither indeed, before thy landing here,   120
Old Siward, with ten thousand warlike men,
All armed at the ready, was setting forth.
Together now we'll better the chance of success
As great as our quarrel is just. Why are you silent?

MACDUFF

Such welcome and unwelcome things at once,   125
'Tis hard to reconcile.

                    Enter Ross

MACDUFF

See who comes here.

MALCOLM

My countryman, but yet I know him not.

MACDUFF

My ever-gentle cousin, welcome hither.

MALCOLM

I know him now. Good God, with speed remove   130
The means that makes us strangers!

ROSS   Sir, amen.

MACDUFF

Stands Scotland where it did?

ROSS   Our poor, poor country,
   Almost afraid to know itself. It cannot
   Be called our mother, but our grave. Where nothing,
   But those who know nothing, are seen to smile;   135
   Where sighs, and groans, and shrieks that rend the air
   Are heard, not heeded; where violent sorrow seems
   A common rhapsody: the dead man's knell
   Rings there but for whom, as good men's lives
   Expire 'fore the flowers wilt in their caps,   140
   Dying before they sicken.

MACDUFF
   O retold all too well, and yet too true.

MALCOLM
   What's the newest grief?

ROSS
   That's an hour past hisses the speaker;
   Each minute teems a new one.

MACDUFF   How does my wife?   145

ROSS
   Why, well.

MACDUFF   And all my children?

ROSS   Well too.

MACDUFF
   The tyrant has not battered at their peace?

ROSS
   No; they were well at peace, when I did leave 'em.

MACDUFF
   Be not a miser with your speech: how goes't?

ROSS
   When I came hither to transport the tidings,   150
   Which heart-broken I have borne, there ran a rumour
   Of many rebellious fellows now armed.

Which I then so witnessed with my own eyes
When I then saw the tyrant's army afoot.
Now's the time for help. Seeing you in Scotland   155
Would create soldiers, make our women fight,
To ditch their dire distresses.

MALCOLM   Be't their comfort,
We are coming there. Gracious England has
Lent us ten thousand men and good Siward:
An older and a better soldier, none that Christendom gives out.

ROSS   Would I could answer 160
This comfort with the like! But I have words,
That would be howled out in the desert air,
Where hearing should not hold them.

MACDUFF   What concern they:
The general cause? Or is it one man's grief,
Due to some single breast?

ROSS   No mind that is just   165
Must in it share some woe, though the main part
Pertains to you alone.

MACDUFF   If it be mine,
Keep it not from me; quickly let me have it.

ROSS

Let not your ears despise my tongue forever,
Which shall possess them with the heaviest sound,   170
That ever yet they heard.

MACDUFF

H'm: I guess at it.

ROSS

Your castle is surprised; your wife, and babes,
Savagely slaughtered. To relate the manner
Were on the bloody mound of these murdered deer   175
To add the death of you.

85

MALCOLM   Merciful Heaven.

    Don't just pull your hat upon your sad brows:
    Give sorrow words; the grief unspoke will ache,
    Whispers the o'er-fraught heart, and bids it break.

MACDUFF

    My children too?   180

ROSS

    Wife, children, servants, all that could be found.

MACDUFF

    And I wasn't home with them? My wife killed too?

ROSS

    I have said.

MALCOLM

    Be comforted.
    Let's make us medicines of our great revenge,   185
    To cure this deadly grief.

MACDUFF

    He has no children. All my pretty ones?
    Did you say all? O Hell-kite! All?
    What, all my pretty chickens, and their dam,
    At one fell swoop?   190

MALCOLM

    Dispute it like a man.

MACDUFF   I shall do so,

    But I must also feel it as a man;
    I can remember things as once they were
    That were most precious to me. Did Heaven look on,
    And would not take their side? Sinful Macduff,   195
    They were all struck for thee. Vile that I am,
    Not for their own demerits, but for mine,
    Slaughter fell on their souls. Heaven rest them now.

MALCOLM

    Be this the whetstone of your sword. Let grief

    Convert to anger; blunt not the heart, enrage it.   200

MACDUFF

    O! I could play the woman with mine eyes,

    And braggart with my tongue. But, gentle Heavens,

    Cut short all intermission. Face to face,

    Bring thou this fiend of Scotland, and myself;

    Within my sword's lethal length set him; if he scape,   205

    Heaven forgive him too!

MALCOLM   This tune goes manly.

    Come, go we to the King; our army is ready;

    Our lack is nothing but our leave. Macbeth

    Is ripe for shaking, and the Powers above

    Put on their instruments. Receive what cheer you may;   210

    His night is long that never sees the day.

Exit

ACT 5 ✦ SCENE 1

DUNSINANE. LADY MACBETH'S PRIVATE ROOMS
IN THE CASTLE

*Enter a Doctor of Physic (a physician as opposed to a titled Cleric)
and a Waiting-Gentle-Woman*

DOCTOR

I have two nights watched with you, but can perceive no
truth in your report. When was it she last sleepwalked?

WOMAN

Since his Majesty went into the field, I have seen her rise
from her bed, throw her nightgown upon her, unlock her
closet, take forth paper, fold it, write upon it, read it, after-   5
wards seal it, and again return to bed; yet all this while in a
most fast sleep.

DOCTOR

A great perturbation in nature, to receive at once the benefit
of sleep, and yet create the appearance of being awake! In
this slumbery agitation, besides her walking and other actual   10
movements, what, at any time, have you heard her say?

WOMAN

That, Sir, which I will not repeat after her.

DOCTOR

You may, to me; and 'tis most fitting you should.

WOMAN

Neither to you, nor any one; having no witness to confirm
my speech.   15

Enter Lady Macbeth, with a taper

Lo you, here she comes. This is her very guise; and, upon my
life, fast asleep. Observe her, stand close.

89

DOCTOR

How came she by that candle?

WOMAN

Why, it sits beside her: she has light by her continually; 'tis
her command.   20

DOCTOR

You see, her eyes are open.

WOMAN

Ay, but their sense are shut.

DOCTOR

What is it she does now? Look, how she rubs her hands.

WOMAN

It is an accustom'd action with her, to seem thus washing
her hands. I have known her continue in this a quarter of   25
an hour.

LADY MACBETH

Yet here's a spot.

DOCTOR

Hark! She speaks. I will write down what comes from her, to
satisfy my remembrance the more strongly.

LADY MACBETH

Out, damned spot! Out, I say! One, two. Why, then 'tis time   30
to do't. Hell is murky. Fie, my Lord, fie, a soldier, and afeard?
What need we fear? Who knows it, when none can call our
power to account? Yet who would have thought the old man
to have had so much blood in him?

DOCTOR

Do you note that?   35

LADY MACBETH

The Thane of Fife had a wife. Where is she now? What, will
these hands ne'er be clean? No more o'that, my Lord, no more
o'that. You mar all with this twitching.

DOCTOR

Come, come; you have known what you should not.

WOMAN

She has spoke what she should not, I am sure of that. Heaven 40
knows what she has known.

LADY MACBETH

Here's the smell of the blood still; all the perfumes of Arabia
will not sweeten this little hand. Oh! Oh! Oh!

DOCTOR

What a sigh is there! The heart is sorely charged.

WOMAN

I would not have such a heart in my bosom, even for the 45
crown that comes with it.

DOCTOR

Well, well, well.

WOMAN

Pray God it be well, sir.

DOCTOR

This disease is beyond my practice: yet I have known those
which have walked in their sleep, who have died holily in 50
their beds.

LADY MACBETH

Wash your hands, put on your nightgown; look not so pale.
I tell you yet again, Banquo's buried; he cannot come out of
his grave.

DOCTOR

Even so? 55

LADY MACBETH

To bed, to bed: there's knocking at the gate. Come, come,
come, come, give me your hand. What's done cannot be
undone. To bed, to bed, to bed.

Exit Lady Macbeth

DOCTOR

Will she go now to bed?

WOMAN

Directly.   60

DOCTOR

Foul whisperings are abroad. Unnatural deeds

Do breed unnatural troubles. Infected minds

To their deaf pillows will discharge their secrets.

More needs she the divine than the physician.

God, God forgive us all. Look after her,   65

Remove from her the means of all self-harm,

And still keep eyes upon her. So, goodnight.

My mind she has baffled, and amazed my sight.

I think, but dare not speak.

WOMAN   Good night, good Doctor.

Exit

ACT 5 ♦ SCENE 2

THE COUNTRY NEAR DUNSINANE

Enter, with drums and colours, Menteith, Caithness, Angus, Lennox,
and Soldiers

MENTEITH

The English army is near, led on by Malcolm,

His uncle Siward *{See-word}* and the good Macduff.

Revenges burn in them; for their dear causes

Would, with its fearsome, bloodthirsty alarm,

Raise up the stone dead man.

ANGUS   Near Birnam wood   5

Shall we well meet them; that way are they coming.

CAITHNESS

Who knows if Donalbain be with his brother?

LENNOX

For certain, Sir, he is not; I have a file
Of all the gentry. There is Siward's son,
And many unrough youths, that only now   10
Assert their sign of manhood.

MENTEITH   What does the tyrant?

CAITHNESS

Great Dunsinane he strongly fortifies.
Some say he's mad; others, that lesser hate him,
Do call it valiant fury: but, for certain,
He cannot buckle his disordered cause   15
Within the belt of rule.

ANGUS   Now does he feel

His secret murders sticking on his hands;
Ev'ry minute revolts reprove his treason:
Those he commands move only in command,
Not for love. Now does he feel his title   20
Hang loose about him, like a giant's robe
Upon a dwarfish thief.

MENTEITH   Who then shall blame

His troubled senses that recoil and flinch,
When all he has within him does condemn
himself, for being there?

CAITHNESS   Well; march we on,   25

To give obedience where 'tis truly owed:
Meet we the medicine for our sick kingdom;
With Malcolm pour we, in our country's purge,
Each drop of us.

LENNOX   Water, much as it needs

To dew the sovereign flower, and drown the weeds,   30
Make we our march towards Birnam.

Exit, marching

93

ACT 5 ◆ SCENE 3

DUNSINANE. A ROOM IN THE CASTLE

Enter Macbeth, Doctor, and Attendants.

MACBETH

Bring me no more reports; let them fly all:
Till Birnam wood remove to Dunsinane,
I cannot pale with fear. What's the boy Malcolm?
Was he not born of woman? The spirits that know
All mortal consequence have pronounced me thus: 5
'Fear not, Macbeth; no man that's born of woman
Shall e'er have power upon thee.' — Then fly, false Thanes,
And mingle with the English libertines;
The mind I sway by, and the heart I bear,
Shall never sag with doubt, nor shake with fear.   10

Enter a Servant

The devil damn thee black, thou cream-faced loon!
Where got'st thou that goose look?

SERVANT

There is ten thousand —

MACBETH   Geese, villain?

SERVANT   Soldiers, Sir.

MACBETH

Go, prick thy face, and make bloody thy fear,
Thou lily-liver'd boy. What soldiers, fool?   15
Death of thy soul, those linen cheeks of thine
Are counsellors to fear. What soldiers, milk-face?

SERVANT

The English force, so please you.

MACBETH

Take thy face hence.

Exit Servant

Seyton! — I am sick at heart,   20

When I behold — Seyton, I say — this push
Will cheer me ever, or dethrone me now.
I have lived long enough: my way of life
Is fallen dry into the desert, the yellow leaf;
And that which should accompany old age,   25
Like honour, love, obedience, troops of friends,
I must not look to have; but in their stead,
Curses, soft but deep, breathing false honour,
Which the heart would gladly deny, but dare not.
Seyton?   30

Enter Seyton

SEYTON
    What's your gracious pleasure?
MACBETH   What news more?
SEYTON
    All is confirmed, my Lord, which was reported.
MACBETH
    I'll fight, till from my bones my flesh be hacked.
    Give me my armour.
SEYTON   'Tis not needed yet.
MACBETH
    I'll put it on.   35
    Send out more horses, skirt the country round,
    Hang those that talk of fear. Give me mine armour.
(to Doctor)
    How does your patient, Doctor?
DOCTOR   Not so sick, my Lord,
    As she is troubled with disturbing visions,
    That keep her from her rest.
MACBETH   Cure her of that.   40
    Canst thou not minister to a mind diseased,
    Pluck from the memory a rooted sorrow,

Raze out the written troubles of the brain,
And with some sweet oblivious antidote
Cleanse the stuffed bosom of that perilous stuff 45
Which weighs upon the heart?

DOCTOR   Therein the patient
Must minister to herself.

MACBETH
Throw potions to the dogs; I'll none of it.
Come, put mine armour on; give me my lance;
Seyton, send out. Doctor, the Thanes fly from me — 50

(to Attendant)
Come, sir, hurry.

(to Doctor)   If thou could, Doctor, test
The water of my land, find her disease,
And purge it to a sound and pristine health,
I'd applaud thee to the very echo,
That should applaud again. — Pull't off, I say. 55
What rhubarb, senna or what purgative drug
Would cleanse these English hence? Hear'st thou of them?

DOCTOR
Ay, my good Lord: your royal preparation
Makes us hear something.

MACBETH
Bring it on to me. 60
I will not be afraid of death and pain,
Till Birnam forest come to Dunsinane.

                    Exit Macbeth

DOCTOR *(aside)*
Were I from Dunsinane away and clear,
Profit again should hardly draw me here.

                    Exit

ACT 5 ◆ SCENE 4

COUNTRY NEAR DUNSINANE WITH BIRNAM WOOD IN VIEW

Enter, with drummers and flag-bearers, (perhaps combining the
flags/colors of Scotland and England), Malcolm, Old Siward, and
Siward's Son — Young Siward, Macduff, Menteith, Caithness, Angus,
Lennox, Ross, and Soldiers, marching

MALCOLM

Cousins, I hope the days are near at hand,

That will be safe in our beds.

MENTEITH   We doubt it nothing.

OLD SIWARD

What wood is this before us?

MENTEITH   The wood of Birnam.

MALCOLM

Let every soldier hew him down a bough,

And bear't before him: thereby shall we conceal   5

The numbers of our men, and make discovery

Falsely in report of us.

SOLDIER

It shall be done.

OLD SIWARD

We learn nothing new other than the confident tyrant

Keeps still in Dunsinane, and will endure   10

Our encampment before't.

MALCOLM   'Tis his main hope;

For where there is advantage to be given,

Both high and low have revolted against him,

And none serve with him but those enforced things,

Whose hearts are absent too.

MACDUFF   Let honest judgment   15

Attend the true outcome, and put we on

Industrious soldiership.

97

OLD SIWARD   The time approaches,
  That will with due decision make us know
  What we shall say we have, and what we owe.
  Speculative thoughts leave unsure hopes to fate,   20
  But for sure results steel must arbitrate:
  Towards which, advance the war.

                    Exit, marching

ACT 5 ♦ SCENE 5

DUNSINANE. WITHIN THE CASTLE

Enter, with drummers and flag-bearers, Macbeth, Seyton,
and Soldiers.

MACBETH

  Hang out our banners on the outward walls;
  The cry is still, 'They come!' Our castle's strength
  Will scoff at any siege: here let them lie,
  Till famine and the fever eat them up.
  Were they not forced with those that should be ours,   5
  We might have met them fearless face to face,
  And beat them fiercely back home.

                    A cry within, of women

                    What is that noise?

SEYTON

  It is the cry of women, my good Lord.

                    Exit Seyton

MACBETH

  I have almost forgot the taste of fears.
  The time has been, my senses would have cooled   10
  To hear a night-shriek; and my head of hair
  Would at a frightening tale stand and stir,
  As life were in't. I have supp'd with slain horrors:
  Such dread, familiar to my slaughterous thoughts,

Cannot startle me. 15

Re-enter Seyton

Wherefore was that cry?

SEYTON

The Queen, my Lord, is dead.

MACBETH

She should have died hereafter;
There would have been a time for such a word.
To-morrow, and to-morrow, and to-morrow, 20
Creeps in this petty pace from day to day,
To the last syllable of recorded time;
And all our yesterdays have lighted fools
The way to dusty death. Out, out, brief candle,
Life's but a walking shadow; a poor player, 25
That struts and frets his hour upon the stage,
And then is heard no more. It is a tale
Told by an idiot, full of sound and fury,
Signifying nothing.

Enter a Messenger

Thou com'st to use thy tongue: thy story quickly. 30

MESSENGER

Gracious my Lord,
I should report that which I say I saw,
But know not how to do't.

MACBETH   Just say, sir.

MESSENGER

As I did stand my watch upon the hill,
I looked toward Birnam, and 'ere long, methought, 35
The wood began to move.

MACBETH   Liar, and slave!

MESSENGER

Let me endure your wrath, if 't be not so.

Within this three mile may you see it coming.
I say, a moving grove.

MACBETH   If thou speak'st false,
Upon the next tree shalt thou hang alive   40
Till famine cling thee. If thy speech be such,
I care not if thou dost for me as much.
I rein in resolution, and begin
To doubt th'equivocation of the Fiend,
That lies like truth: 'Fear not, till Birnam wood   45
Do come to Dunsinane', and now a wood
Comes toward Dunsinane. Arm, arm, and fight.
If this which he avouches does appear,
There is no flying hence, nor tarrying here.
I 'gin to be aweary of the sun,   50
And wish th'estate o'th'world were now undone.
Ring the alarm bell. Blow, wind! Come, wrack!
At least we'll die with harness on our back.

Exit

ACT 5 ◆ SCENE 6

THE SAME. A PLAIN BEFORE THE CASTLE

Enter, with drummers and flag-bearers, Malcolm, Old Siward,
Macduff, and their army, with branches & boughs

MALCOLM

Now, near enough: your leafy screens throw down,
And show like those you are. You, worthy uncle,
Shall, with my cousin, your right noble son,
Lead our first battle. Worthy Macduff, and we,
Shall take upon's what else remains to do,   5
According to our order.

OLD SIWARD   Fare you well.
Do we but find the tyrant's power tonight,

Let us be beaten, if we cannot fight.

MACDUFF

Make all our trumpets speak; give them all breath,

Those clamorous harbingers of blood and death.   10

Exit. Alarms continued

ACT 5 ◆ SCENE 7

THE SAME. ANOTHER PART OF THE PLAIN

Enter Macbeth

MACBETH

They have tied me to a stake: I cannot fly,

But, bear-like, I must fight the course. What's he,

That was not born of woman? Such a one

Am I to fear, or none.

Enter Young Siward

YOUNG SIWARD

What is thy name?   5

MACBETH

Thou'lt be afraid to hear it.

YOUNG SIWARD

 No; though thou call'st thyself a hotter name

Than any is in hell.

MACBETH   My name's Macbeth.

YOUNG SIWARD

The devil himself could not pronounce a title

More hateful to mine ear.

MACBETH   No, nor more fearful.   10

YOUNG SIWARD

Thou liest, abhorred tyrant: with my sword

I'll prove the lie thou speak'st.

They fight, and Young Siward is slain

MACBETH

    Thou wast born of woman:

    But swords I smile at, weapons laugh to scorn,

    Brandished by man that's of a woman born.   15

Exit Macbeth

Alarms. Enter Macduff

MACDUFF

    That way the noise is. Tyrant, show thy face,

    If thou be'st slain, and with no stroke of mine,

    My wife and children's ghosts will haunt me still.

    I cannot strike at wretched men, whose arms

    Are hired to bear their lances: either thou, Macbeth,   20

    Or else my sword, with an unbloodied edge,

    I sheathe again undeeded. There thou shouldst be;

    By this great clatter, one of greatest note

    Seems proclaimed. Let me find him, Fortune,

    And more I beg not.   25

Exit Macduff. Alarm

Enter Malcolm and Old Siward

OLD SIWARD

    This way, my Lord, the castle's gently rendered.

    The tyrant's people on both sides do fight;

    The noble Thanes do bravely in the war.

    The day almost give's itself to you,

    And little is to do.

MALCOLM   We have met with foes   30

    Who as friends will not strike us.

OLD SIWARD   Enter, Sir.

They enter the castle

Exit. Alarm

ACT 5 ◆ SCENE 8

ANOTHER PART OF THE FIELD

Enter Macbeth.

MACBETH

    Why should I play the Roman fool, and die

    On mine own sword? Whiles I see the living,

    Gashes I will grant them.

                    Re-enter Macduff

MACDUFF   Turn, Hell-hound, turn!

MACBETH

    Of all men else I have avoided thee.

    But get thee back, my soul is too much charged   5

    With blood of thine already.

MACDUFF   I have no words.

    My voice is in my sword: thou bloodier villain

    Than words can call thee out!

                      They fight

MACBETH   Thou wastes thy work,

    As if blindly thrusting thy keen sword

    through the vaporous air, to make me bleed.   10

    Let fall thy blade on vulnerable crests;

    I bear a charméd life, which must not yield

    To one of woman born.

MACDUFF   Despair thy charm,

    And let the Devil, whom thou still hast served,

    Tell thee, Macduff was from his mother's womb   15

    Untimely ripped.

MACBETH

    Accurséd be that tongue that tells me so,

    For it hath cowed my very manliness.

    And be these midnight hags no more believed,

    That deal false with us in a double sense,   20

That keep the word of promise to our ear,
And break it to our hope. I'll not fight with thee.

MACDUFF

Then yield thee, coward,
And live to be the laughing stock o'th'time.
We'll have thee, as our rarer monsters are,   25
Blazed on a banner, and written below:
'Here may you see the tyrant.'

MACBETH   I will not yield
To kiss the ground before young Malcolm's feet,
And to be baited with the rabble's curse.
Though Birnam wood be come to Dunsinane,   30
And thou, my foe, being of no woman born,
Yet I will try the last. Before my body
I throw my warlike shield. Lay on, Macduff,
And damned be him that first cries, 'Hold, enough!'

Exit, fighting. Alarms. Re-enter fighting, and MACBETH slain.
Exit MACDUFF with MACBETH's body

ACT 5 ◆ SCENE 9

WITHIN THE CASTLE

Retreat. Flourish. Enter, with drummers and flag-bearers, Malcolm,
Old Siward, Ross, Thanes, and Soldiers

MALCOLM

I would the friends we miss were safe arrived.

OLD SIWARD

Some have died here; and yet, by these I see,
So great a day as this is worth such loss.

MALCOLM

Macduff is missing, and your noble son.

ROSS

Your son, my Lord, has paid a soldier's debt: 5

He only lived but till he was a man,
The which no sooner had his prowess confirmed,
By the unyielding way in which he fought,
And like a man he died.
OLD SIWARD   Then he is dead?
ROSS
Ay, and brought off the field. Your cause of sorrow   10
Must not be measur'd by his worth, for then
It hath no end.
OLD SIWARD   Had he his wounds in front?
ROSS
Ay, on the front.
OLD SIWARD   Why then, God's soldier be he!
Had I as many sons as I have hairs,
I would not wish them to a fairer death.   15
And so, his knell is knolled.
MALCOLM   He's worth more sorrow,
And that I'll spend for him.
OLD SIWARD   He's worth no more.
They say he parted well and paid his score,
And so God be with him! Here comes newer comfort.
            Re-enter Macduff, with Macbeth's head

MACDUFF
Hail, King! for so thou art. Behold, where stands   20
Th'usurper's cursed head: the time is free.
I see thee circled by thy kingdom's pearl,
That speak my salutation in their minds;
Whose voices I desire aloud with mine.
Hail, King of Scotland.   25
ALL
Hail, King of Scotland!

A Flourish of trumpets. As Malcolm speaks, the Three Witches enter
holding Fleance by the hand. They all wear crowns of garland. The
ghost of Banquo enters with them and stands behind his son, places
a hand on his shoulder and They watch and listen.

MALCOLM

We shall not spend a large expense of time,
Before we reckon with your several loves
And make us even with you. My Thanes and kinsmen,
Henceforth be Earls; the first that ever Scotland   30
In such an honour named. What we must do,
Is to plant anew in this freed earth,
By calling home our exiled friends abroad,
Who fled the snares of watchful tyranny.
Then bring forth to justice the cruel ministers   35

(holding up Macbeth's head)

Of this dead butcher, and his fiend-like Queen,
Who, as 'tis thought, by self and violent hands
Took her own life. This, and what needful else
That calls upon us, by the grace of Grace,
We will perform in measure, time, and place.   40
So thanks to all at once, whom by next moon,
Here we invite to see us crowned at Scone. *{Skoon}*

WITCH 1

So thanks to all at once,

WITCH 2

Who by next moon,

WITCH 3

Thee, we invite to see —   45

FLEANCE

Who will be crowned at Scone?

ACT 5 ◆ SCENE 9

Flourish of trumpets. The Witches and Fleance run about the crowd and play "murder and coronation" as the Others Exit. Banquo's Ghost follows Malcolm off.

FINIS

OR

THE END FOR NOW